It's a LONGway DOWN to the TOP

A Book for the Comfortable Christian

Pressing on to the Depths of
the Divine Viewpoint

David H. Stroud

WestBow
PRESS
A DIVISION OF THOMAS NELSON

T0171548

ISBN: 978-1-4497-6962-8 (sc)
ISBN: 978-1-4497-6963-5 (hc)
ISBN: 978-1-4497-6961-1 (e)

Library of Congress Control Number: 2012919223

WestBow Press books may be ordered through booksellers or by contacting:

WestBow Press
A Division of Thomas Nelson
1663 Liberty Drive
Bloomington, IN 47403
www.westbowpress.com
1-(866) 928-1240

Printed in the United States of America

WestBow Press rev. date 11/7/2012:

Dedicated to Dr. Troy S. Welch,
President and Founder,
Channel Islands Bible College and Seminary,
Man of God

━━━━━━━━

CONTENTS

PREFACE

PERHAPS IT IS NOT THE EXPERIENCE of all believing Christians, but the striking conviction of how far Jesus calls His followers to go when He asks them to leave the life they had been living up to the point of rebirth has always been, for me, one of the most powerful influences of the Holy Spirit. To be sure, this has not been a pleasant experience in many ways, but the other powerful influences springing from the enormous nature of the One who calls lessen any harshness or tendency to retreat to the temporary ease of the world. Our God is very great, and His love is beyond any human evaluation of what is worthwhile; it is worth everything we are and everything He has given us. Jesus said that His food was to do the will of the Father who sent Him and to finish His Father's work. I hope that this book can be food for the reader. Honestly, I have had to read this repeatedly to remind myself of the call of Christ and its great scope—right up the frontiers of my fear of the unknown and the hesitancy within my growing faith.

INTRODUCTION

"'Come now, and let us reason together,
says the Lord" (Isa. 1:18).

THIS VERSE TELLS US THAT THE reasoning is true, and if the reasoning is as true as God is true, our habit of looking at our world and ourselves the way we prefer will be revealed. Let's not ignore our pride and insecurity for a pleasant picture of ourselves that we use to delay reasoning together with the Lord. God's perfect love will cast out our fear of the truth about life.

"The Lord is gracious and full of compassion, slow to anger and great in mercy. The Lord is good to all, and His tender mercies are over all His works" (Ps. 145:7–8).

My intent is to build familiarity with the restraint the Holy Spirit places on believers facing the temptations of this world and to remove the blinders from believers, allowing them to see the Creator everywhere. Whichever image affects the reader, I feel an urgency to deliver this message before the rapture of the Lord's church. Love lived out in faith is the rule. The time for messing around has passed; we no longer have the luxury of wasting time. "Certainly not! How shall we who died to sin live any longer in it?" (Rom. 6:2).

What is our frame of reference surrounding our view of what's carnal and what's spiritual in our lives? Is it our personal lives since we first believed? Is it life since conception? Is it the church age? Is it Noah to 2012? Is it Genesis 1:2 up to and beyond Revelation 22:6?

Is it what other Christians think? Is it what we've verified in the Bible? The focus of this book is to form and encourage a frame of reference, a viewpoint for comparison rooted in the garden of Eden and the kingdom of heaven. Though the difference between the here and now and the ends (the garden and heaven) is drastic, this viewpoint can counter our tendency to alter righteous guidelines, even biblical doctrine, in favor of a less-than-pure compromise. Are we willing to live uncompromised lives all the way to the edge, all the way to the very framework, the boundaries of our viewpoint? If indeed our point of view can be pictured as being surrounded by a frame of reference, let us imagine a seven sided frame of biblical instruction:

Side one:

"Now godliness with contentment is great gain. And having food and clothing, with these we shall be content" (1 Tim. 6:8).

"Now to Him who is able to do exceedingly abundantly above all that we ask or think, according to the power that works in us, to Him be glory in the church by Christ Jesus to all generations, forever and ever. Amen" (Eph. 3:20).

Side two:

"Jesus said unto him, 'Foxes have holes, and birds of the air have nests; but the Son of man has nowhere to lay his head'" (Luke 9:58).

"When you give a dinner or a supper, do not ask your friends, your brothers, your relatives, nor rich neighbors, lest they also invite you back, and you be repaid. But when you give a feast, invite the poor, the maimed, the lame, the blind. And you will be blessed, because they cannot repay you; for you shall be repaid at the resurrection of the just" (Luke 14:12–13).

"That Christ may dwell in your hearts through faith." (Eph. 3:17) "For where your treasure is, there your heart will be also" (Matt. 6:21).

Side three:

"But when you are invited, go and sit down in the lowest place" (Luke 14:10).

"And whoever exalts himself will be humbled, and he who humbles himself will be exalted" (Matt. 23:12). "So the last will be first, and the first last" (Matt. 20:16).

Side four:

"For you were once darkness, but now you are light in the Lord. Walk as children of light" (Eph. 5:8).

"And have no fellowship with the unfruitful works of darkness … For it is shameful even to speak of those things which are done by them in secret" (Eph. 5:11–12).

Side five:

"O Lord, I know the way of man is not in himself; it is not in man who walks to direct his own steps" (Jer. 10:23).

"Show me Your ways, O Lord; teach me Your paths. Lead me in Your truth and teach me, for You are the God of my salvation; on You I wait all the day" (Ps. 25:4–5).

Side six:

"We are fools for Christ's sake, but you are wise in Christ! We are weak, but you are strong! You are distinguished, but we are dishonored! … We have been made as the filth of the world, the offscouring of all things until now" (1 Cor. 4:10, 13).

"Or do you not know that your body is the temple of the Holy Spirit who is in you, whom you have from God, and you are not your own? For you were bought at a price; therefore glorify God in your body and in your spirit, which are God's" (1 Cor. 6:19–20).

Side seven:
"Give us help from trouble, for the help of man is useless" (Ps. 60:11).
"All my springs are in You" (Ps. 87:7).

At the beginning and the end of the Bible are descriptions of what sounds like heaven on earth in Eden and the new heaven and the new earth to come. I endeavor to keep the nature and character of God central in any conception of the nature of Eden and heaven. Whether my endeavors meet with the reader's approval is not within my control. I also assume that the reader knows that by way of Adam's sin the world is now under the sway of Satan and his demons. By the atoning death of Jesus the Christ, the enemy's power over believers is broken, and his rule over the world will end when Christ comes to reign in his place. This will happen when the earth as we know it ceases to exist, and the sin overshadowing us will vanish in the kingdom of heaven. In this book, I offer opinions built on comparison and deduction, using biblical information about history, sin, prophecy, and the mind of Christ, as well as recorded secular history.

IT'S A LONG WAY
DOWN TO THE TOP

---

*N*OT TO PUT TOO FINE OF a point on it, but do we humans "not know that [we] are wretched, miserable, poor, blind, and naked"? (Rev. 3:17).

In His revelation, the Lord Jesus is speaking to all who need to hear, but this verse is bizarre, considering that the specific people He addressed are believers and appeared to be "rich, have become wealthy, and have need of nothing" (Rev. 3:17).

The core of this message to immature saints and certainly to those without faith is that they "do not know" and do not see.

The truth of God is solid and the love of God is constant, and both traits are clear when we see how God relentlessly works toward the time when "the eyes of your understanding being enlightened; that you may know what is the hope of His calling, what are the riches of the glory of His inheritance in the saints" (Eph. 1:18).

This spiritual change allowing holy comprehension in the human heart confirms Christ's revelation that indeed "the kingdom of God is within you" (Luke 17:21) and "surely the kingdom of God has come upon you" (Luke 11:20).

We are called to look for this kingdom of God here and now as well as then, up yonder.

How were we before the fall, and how will we be in heaven? I pose these questions beside a view of how we have done throughout history, a spiritual and physical comparison using biblical revelation and sanctified deduction.

Can we make reasonable comparisons and evolutionary deductions from the nature and result of sin in human history by looking at biblical revelation about man before the fall and about the coming kingdom of heaven? Have we really progressed as modern advances would seem to indicate, or have form (self-image) and function (faster) buried and blinded us?

In the brief account of life in the garden of Eden, we see that simplicity and peace with God were clear foundations of existence at that time. In very stark contrast, modern life is crowded, complex, and steadily becomes more and more selfish, futile, and clamorous. What it was like to live in Eden is difficult to imagine, let alone truly experience. No matter how quiet, serene, peaceful, and beautiful the setting we may find, we can't escape ourselves. To be sure, Eden is impossible for us achieve because our rebellion against God continually taints everything in us and around us. "O wretched [race] that [we are]! Who will deliver [us] from this body of death?" (Rom. 7:24).

In an amazing statement about mankind's fall to spiritual death and continuing physical decay, we learn that earth is tied to our sin, death, redemption, and resurrection.

> *For the earnest expectation of the creation eagerly waits for the revealing of the sons of God. For the creation was subjected to futility, not willingly, but because of Him who subjected it in hope; because the creation itself also will be delivered from the bondage of corruption into the glorious liberty of the children of God. For we know that the whole creation groans and labors with birth pangs together until now. Not only that, but we also who have the firstfruits of the Spirit, even we ourselves groan within ourselves, eagerly waiting for the adoption, the redemption of our body.*

—*Rom. 8:19–23*

Our willful unbelief about our connection to the corruption of creation is a major concern of this book, as is the beautiful connection to the Lord of creation for those who choose to live in Christ. "For those who live according to the flesh set their minds on the things of the flesh, but those who live according to the Spirit, the things of the Spirit. For to be carnally minded is death, but to be spiritually minded is life and peace" (Rom. 8:5–6).

The kingdom of heaven is described and spiritually discerned as that which seems to be the opposite of what man has created. It is perhaps the perfected completion of what the garden of Eden was meant to be. But we don't really know because Jesus says, "Behold, I make all things new" (Rev. 21:5), and the apostle John says, "I saw a new heaven and a new earth, for the first heaven and the first earth had passed away" (Rev. 21:1).

Is heaven an unimaginably different new reality or, at the very least, an unimaginably new "us" perceiving in a way we could never before imagine? "It is written: 'Eye has not seen, nor ear heard, nor have entered into the heart of man the things which God has prepared for those who love Him.'" (1 Cor. 2:9).

We shall see. We ride a runaway train from a painful point of departure from true bliss and are speeding toward a destination of a new joyful life with the risen Christ—or not. The Holy Scriptures make clear who will survive the crash and who will be rescued before it happens.

Here we are in the middle between the point of departure from the garden and the destination in heaven, and multitudes ask, "Where are we? Where did we come from? Why are we here? What is right? Where are we going? What does this all mean?" Still more multitudes could not care less, and more don't even ask or even think to. "So what? How does this matter?"

We are told, "Look to Me, and be saved, all you ends of the earth! For I am God, and there is no other" (Isa. 45:22) and to keep focused on "Jesus, the author and finisher of our faith" (Heb. 12:2), knowing He is our wisdom, our peace, and our completion, but we are still here in the middle. Humanity has spent a long time in sin since the fall, but we have been mercifully spared and allowed to try to make it somehow.

Here in the life we have made, we must not ignore the world into which the Lord Jesus has sent us. We don't always recognize the waywardness of the world, but spiritual growth can allow us to discern the selfishness and sin that are so much a part of what we see and do. The light of salvation looks brighter when the darkness is correctly perceived, and vice versa. How much we have become enmeshed in sin, and how much evidence of sin there is! How much evidence of the beautiful Holy God there is, and how the church has grown in numbers!

We must see both sides. Our view involves a choice. We are forgiven, and cleansing is more available than the air we breathe. Therefore let us choose not to dwell only on the dark that the light of God has allowed us to see in our lives, no matter how "normal" it appears.

CREATION AND THE GARDEN

---

*T*HESE THOUGHTS ON THE GARDEN AND heaven are imaginings. The "imaginer" is a regenerated, believing man with an old sinful nature. These imaginings are by no means as extensive, deep, or complete as they could be and don't touch all the bases they could. I hope that they inspire discernment and meditation in the church—those seeking the difficult way to the narrow gate with few souls on it in the midst of the broad way to destruction taken by far too many souls. The narrow way is lit only as far as a lamp lights the path for walking feet. Therefore it is good to "watch" (Mark 13:37). "Your word is a lamp to my feet and a light to my path" (Ps. 119:105).

God said, "Let there be light" … And God saw the light, that it was good. God said, "Let the waters under the heavens be gathered together into one place, and let the dry land appear"; and it was so. And God called the dry land Earth, and the gathering together of the waters He called Seas … And God saw that it was good.

God said, "Let the earth bring forth grass, the herb that yields seed, and the fruit tree that yields fruit according to its kind, whose seed is in itself, on the earth" … And God saw that it was good.

God said, "Let there be lights in the firmament of the heavens to divide the day from the night; and let them be for signs and seasons, and for days and years; and let them be for lights in the firmament of the heavens to give light on the earth" … And God saw that it was good.

God said, "Let the waters abound with an abundance of living creatures, and let birds fly above the earth across the face of the firmament of the heavens." … And God saw that it was good.

God said, "Let the earth bring forth the living creature according to its kind: cattle and creeping thing and beast of the earth, each according to its kind" … And God saw that it was good.

Then God said, "Let Us make man in Our image, according to Our likeness; let them have dominion over the fish of the sea, over the birds of the air, and over the cattle, over all the earth and over every creeping thing that creeps on the earth." So God created man in His own image; in the image of God He created him; male and female He created them. Then God blessed them, and God said to them, "Be fruitful and multiply; fill the earth and subdue it; have dominion over the fish of the sea, over the birds of the air, and over every living thing that moves on the earth." And God said, "See, I have given you every herb that yields seed which is on the face of all the earth, and every tree whose fruit yields seed; to you it shall be for food. Also, to every beast of the earth, to every bird of the air, and to everything that creeps on the earth, in which there is life, I have given every green herb for food"; and it was so. Then God saw everything that He had made, and indeed it was very good.

—Gen. 1: 3–4, 9–12, 20–21, 24–31

There can be no doubt that the habitation for mankind that the Lord brought into being was no less than perfect and complete. His desire to love mankind with all that He is becomes crystal clear and lights up the pages of scripture with the words of His blessing of the man and the woman. This is God Who is smiling upon us. That God judges His creation to be very good indeed means far more than the evaluation any human could make. When God says it is good, it is good in a dimension we cannot sense or fully appreciate because we don't live in that dimension … yet.

The fact that God blessed what He had made shows that it was to be above and beyond sufficient in every way and deeply delightful to the inhabitants. It also appears that man was to live without eating dead animate life; that is, he was to have a vegan diet. Death is messy and tragic, no matter whose life is ended, and God said that "every herb" and "every tree whose fruit yields seed … to you it shall be for food." At this point in history, food was plant life, not anything from the animal kingdom. It seems this food was clean, peaceful, abundant, and as reliable as God Himself.

The difference between the creation of man and the creation of everything else is that man was formed out of a substance created before him—the "dust," or earth. Special attention and blessing were bestowed on man in that the Lord "breathed into his nostrils the breath of life; and man became a living being."

God created man by hand-forming him and putting within him His breath, His Spirit. The Hebrew word for *breath* is *ruach,* which is the same word for *Spirit*; like the ancient Greek word *pneuma* and the Latin *spiritus.* The last section of this verse can also be translated "and man became a living soul." This seems to indicate that man *is* a living soul. However, 1 Thessalonians 5:23 reads, "Now may the God of peace Himself sanctify you completely; and may your whole spirit, soul, and body be preserved blameless at the coming of our Lord Jesus Christ."

This verse teaches that man *possesses* a soul as part of his essence. Having been made out of dust, man, like all other life forms, is somehow tied to creation and to the planet. Scripture says that "the creation itself also will be delivered from the bondage of corruption into the glorious liberty of the children of God" (Rom. 8:21).

In describing the difference between Adam and Christ, Paul refers to the man of the earth as the "man of dust" and says "the second Man is the Lord from heaven," namely the "heavenly Man" (1 Cor. 15:45–49). Death had not entered the "man of dust" or the world until the fall, so it seems that even man's relation to his surroundings had a spiritual component that today's men, even the creation-worshipers, can only hope for. It appears there was no "self" within Adam separating him from anything, especially the Lord.

Now, we are selfish, and if we compare the strength of the Evil One to our strength without Christ, we can get an image of just how selfish we are—overly selfish, if that is possible. Our self-centeredness is something we think, we buy, we save for, we dress in, we eat, we measure against others, we judge in others, we deny in ourselves, and teach to others, and we retreat from the Savior's judgment of it in us. To overcome our selfishness, we must follow the Lord away from ourselves, desiring Him exceedingly above all we could ask for or imagine. When God recreates us and all that Adam had started, with the glory of the Lord Jesus in us and in the world, what man has hoped for will finally be a full, overwhelming reality.

So in the beginning, man was made in the image of God; had a body, soul, and spirit; was given dominion over all creation, and was "kissed" by God when He breathed the divine Spirit into him. Wow! We are the crown of creation. Do you feel like the crown of creation?

But it gets better. The Lord of the whole universe Himself planted a garden and put man in it, giving him his "home."

"And out of the ground the Lord God made every tree grow that is pleasant to the sight and good for food." Also, "a river went out of Eden to water the garden" (Gen. 2:8, 10).

In today's world there is a multitude of edible vegetables and fruits, even if you don't count the breeding manipulation that has given rise to a far greater variety. With no sin or death in the world, the term *organic* can be applied only to the creation era, in the strictest sense.

The Merriam-Webster Dictionary defines *paradise* in reference to Eden as "a place of pristine or abundant natural beauty." Amazingly, it appears that the weather was pristine as well. "For the Lord God had not caused it to rain on the earth, and there was no man to till the ground; but a mist went up from the earth and watered the whole face of the ground" (Gen. 2:5).

With no precipitation needed to sustain life, it sounds like the weather was perfect all day, every day.

"Then the Lord God took the man and put him in the garden of Eden to tend and keep it" (Gen. 2:15). This is the only verse in the book of Genesis describing man's activity before the fall outside of being fruitful and multiplying. (Reproduction would imply the creation of families, and parenting.) But as an activity that is a "duty," what exactly does tending the garden mean? Modern gardens need weeding, pruning, protecting, soil care, and the discarding of dead material. Even the care of forests has some of these components. Did Eden have plants that died? Was population control necessary? Were there weeds? Probably not.

"Therefore, just as through one man sin entered the world, and death through sin, … thus death spread to all men, because all sinned" (Rom 5:12). Does this verse mean that only men began to die as a result of Adam's sin, or was creation eternally complete and perfect then too, not suffering from age or death? Plants and animals that do not decay or die? Just a thought for the future.

Considering what we are now and picturing the possibility of tending the beautiful garden with the Lord God Almighty in person as Father and friend, we might easily imagine boredom setting in. Was the Lord bored when He created everything? Was He bored after He finished? Is the Lord ever bored? Is boredom a distinct product of the fall? Another thought for the future.

The Lord, who is three perfectly related persons in one God, probably did not want us to live alone in paradise. Adam was blessed by the other life forms around him. They were probably not dangerous and perhaps were even good company. This changed after the fall and after the flood.

"And the fear of you and the dread of you shall be on every beast of the earth, on every bird of the air, on all that move on the earth, and on all the fish of the sea. They are given into your hand" (Gen. 9:2).

Having been alone for a time, Adam must have experienced a growing need for companionship. The Lord knew his heart and knew his need. Adam got company.

The best news since the creation of everything else before was the formation out of man of woman—the perfect, beautiful half of the crown of creation. Thank you, Lord, for the divine joining of man and woman, which is central in our existence!

"Then God blessed them, and God said to them, 'Be fruitful and multiply; fill the earth and subdue it; have dominion over the fish of the sea, over the birds of the air, and over every living thing that moves on the earth'" (Gen. 1:28). This is a clear revelation from the Lord that His creation was to be filled with those whom He loved to share it with! What we grope for nowadays is a self-absorbed deviation from God's original intention. This is pitiful; our "evolved" desires can never be compared with natural perfection and completion in pristine existence with our Creator. Most of us are not looking for the Creator in order to enjoy what He has to share with us. After all, what's in it for us? The life He offers is boring!

Nevertheless, we did multiply fruitfully, increasing exceedingly and replenishing the earth. Trying to see by faith to contemplate mankind multiplying and bearing only the fruit of the Spirit is difficult, considering our history of separation and war. In fact, it seems that we have sown the lust of the flesh and reaped accordingly as we filled the planet.

Offering a complete contrast with current reality, the Bible tells us that the Lord God made "woman, and He brought her to the man … Therefore a man shall leave his father and mother and be joined to his wife, and they shall become one flesh. And they were both naked, the man and his wife, and were not ashamed" (Gen. 2:22, 24–25).

A lack of shame over living without clothes is radically opposed to today's view, but it also points to life in an environment where men and women could exist without clothing and be in no danger.

Amazing! Man and woman could sleep out in the open, eat good food, swim in the river, and explore and tend the garden of the living God, who was present in physical form ("And they heard the sound of the Lord God walking in the garden in the cool of the day," Gen 3:8), as friend, companion, guide, teacher, and parent. They lived totally in the present with wide open minds and hearts overflowing with joy and love because there was nothing but joy and love everywhere. Wow! It is hard to fully imagine the reality of this because we are essentially unable now. We are infected, troubled, and limited by inherent sin.

To have dominion over the earth as God intended entails a guardianship over the whole beautiful world. This guardianship is the type that all environmentalists, particularly the most fanatical, dream of and attempt to practice. The catch is that, even with all their noble intentions and heartfelt commitment to living on the earth as God intended, they are not able to change their own hearts to restore the purity that existed before the fall. The infection that has wreaked havoc on the environment has enfeebled them, too.

Even the most environmentally oriented people struggle with hearts that sin in self-centeredness. All real lasting change in our environment must come from within us first. The heart of man must change in the most profound way. He must accept death to self by giving up his right to himself, his answers, and his agenda and seek the Creator with His power and His plan for change.

Certainly man has been responsible for vast restorative as well as destructive environmental change, but almost every effort to encourage humanity's healthy dominion over the creation has been hindered by division between people, even within the environmental movement. Environmentalists hold an "us versus them" position toward the "destroyers," and vice versa. "Imagine all of us caring about how we treat the earth as if our very lives and our descendants' lives depended on it," environmentalists say. These are noble principles to live by, but we are incredibly selfish.

If anyone says he is not selfish, or at least not *that* selfish, that's a good indication he is. Selfishness separates us, and separation hinders or stops man's efforts. The heart must be the first place for re-creation by the Lord. That change then extends to other hearts and then to the whole of creation.

Talk is cheap and human effort is futile compared with the permanent change brought through reborn hearts. A new heart costs the life of the Son of God, and every true believer in Christ knows it costs the right to his own life. Nothing short of that radical foundational change will be of any lasting consequence. This is the standard that Christ has set. It is unattainable without God, and the apostle Paul said even he had not understood this. This is real change. As the true author of faith, who begins the re-creation of men, and ultimately the re-creation of this world where we will live, Jesus is thus the greatest and only permanently effective environmentalist.

The Bible does not say how long the beautiful life in Eden lasted, but that it happened at all is way more than enough, even considering how little detail we have. Experience shows that rebirth in Christ yields spiritual babies, and it seems that it would have been the same here. The Lord has always referred to us as children and Himself as Father, especially in the words of God the Son. We are like the struggling infant in the first dozen verses of Ezekiel 16. By contrast, the first man and woman appear to have had perfection at first, though certainly not later.

With the tree of life and the tree of the knowledge of good and evil growing in the garden, it appears the Lord had a purpose for both trees in relation to humanity. Clearly the fruit of the tree of knowledge was not to be eaten, but even to have it there seems to indicate that God intended to provide Adam and Eve with the knowledge of good and evil perhaps in a more gradual way. We can only guess. Looking to Jesus and His teachings guides us to knowledge of good and evil. Will we have perfect knowledge in heaven? In any case, the premature ingestion of the knowledge of good and evil took place, and that beautiful life in Eden ended.

What would it be like to live without any consciousness of good as opposed to evil? Would everything be good? How great it would be not to have any useless clutter, to have no possibility but the good Lord and the wonderful existence He maintains in abundance! It was great then, and it will be even better for sure.

But back to Eden, and enter the enemy of our souls, Satan, the accuser, as a serpent, and a talking serpent at that. The "serpent" most likely did not look like a snake as we know it. It is more likely that he had an appearance that did not alarm Eve or arouse her suspicion. "And no wonder! For Satan himself transforms himself into an angel of light" (2 Cor. 11:14).

This creature is pure self-centeredness taken to its most despicable extreme. Wanting to usurp the throne of God, he knows he cannot, so his focus is on destroying the Lord's children. Cowardly but shrewd, he brings the first notion of selfishness into the mind of Eve. Using his keen perception that the fruit of the tree of the knowledge of good and evil is a strong enticement, he then injects the first experience of falsehood and deception into the mind and heart of Adam's wife, who before was pure, and left alone, was incapable of these notions.

Incredibly claiming that God lied by saying that death would follow if she ate the fruit, the Evil One overwhelms her with the notion that she could be like God and see like Him if she knew good and evil. This twisted con job makes the Lord into a liar (which He never is) and much less than absolutely good (which He always is).

This enemy is truly worthy of all our hatred. He infected us with his disease and gives us regular booster shots to make the illness worse, generation after generation. Eve was unprepared, and bowled over by a slippery sleazy liar, she did the unthinkable, at least from our viewpoint. Would we have done the same thing if we had lived as the first humans did up until the first sin? Will your submission to God provide the answer, or will your pride?

The depth of the next wounds inflicted by this encounter is revealed to us only by the Holy Spirit. The first woman, totally taken advantage of by the enemy, consumed the knowledge of good and evil way too soon and offered her husband some. Adam ate, but he was not deceived; he sinned with his eyes open and knew just what he was doing—rebelling against God and essentially telling Him, "I will do what I want."

It appears that the effect was immediate, and both Adam and Eve were suddenly aware that they were naked. This is described in a number of ways by those who study the Scriptures.

"Who cover Yourself with light as with a garment, Who stretch out the heavens like a curtain" (Ps. 104:2). "He was transfigured before them. His face shone like the sun, and His clothes became as white as the light" (Matt. 17:2).

These verses about God have led some to think that Adam and Eve may have been clothed in light and that at the point of their sin the light went out. However it happened, their perception of themselves as naked was a complete surprise. They saw themselves exposed by the wrong they had done and recoiled into the first hiding.

It would not be much of a stretch to say that to Adam and Eve everything looked different, because everything was definitely different from then on. Falling further, they heard the Lord coming and pitifully tried to hide from God while trying to hide from what they had done; mostly they were trying to hide from what they had now become.

Probably the worst feeling in existence now entered the first humans: fear. They were afraid of God, and His voice prompted in them the urge to hide from Him. Many people can recall the first time they were afraid of their father or mother, though they may not consider what it would have been like never to have to fear their parents.

This concept of a fearless life is absolutely foreign to modern man. We are steeped in fear, and it is built in now. It could be dared to proclaim that we cannot conceive of what the absence of fear is like. Fear has had such a sweeping influence over our history that it cannot be overstated. From the subtle chill to terror-stricken paralysis, fear is our biggest affliction. From the time of the fall, our plague, without Jesus, is the fear of death.

In His interrogation of Adam, Eve, and the serpent, God laid bare the deception and the rebellion, declaring the curses and putting them into effect. The plan of redemption from long before, known only to God, was now revealed, but not in its entirety. Satan, as a defeated foe, was cursed to eating dust, and the seed of the woman would ultimately curse him to eating fire forever in everlasting defeat. The Savior would in all respects eliminate the enemy's existence for humanity.

The magnitude of the change that took place in our original parents with the fall cannot be adequately expressed. To say that they experienced guilt, shame, remorse, and loss is correct but does not convey what was absolutely the worst experience in the history of mankind. Did they even come to wish for death right then or later? Did the immense, radical change they experienced foretell the immense, radical change that would reverse the fall—the resurrection to everlasting life with Jesus? In any case, the poor newborn sinners must have been very depressed and terrorized.

The Bible tells us that God expelled Adam and Eve from the garden so that they would not eat of the tree of life and have to live forever, hopelessly separated from Him. Scripture also does not clearly state that the Lord explained this to them before He kicked them out. This must have been the darkest day for people who had known no spiritual darkness until this terrible chain of events. I have been asked to leave, and I have been told to leave; lots of people have had the same experience. Multiply that by what must have seemed like infinity, and you might get a glimpse of their broken hearts and the beginning of our indescribably serious state of sin.

What was this out-on-the-streets transition like for the two beginners? Because the Lord remains true, our first parents were not abandoned; far from it. "I will be with you. I will not leave you nor forsake you" (Josh. 1:5).

If God has told *us* this, how much more would He cling to those two who were painfully scorched by the first baptism of fire, entering into sin and death, which they brought upon themselves and which man has experienced ever since? The world was still abundantly supplied with everything they needed to live, multiply, and even prosper. God still was close and had not removed His love, mercy, grace, and generosity from them. He was just as He is today. Look for Him and He is everywhere, tolerant of the mess we have made and living in the hearts of men and women.

The first human children must have had the most profound impact on Adam and Eve. What better way to shower them with love than with the first baby. Imagine that—the first baby! How much the Lord showed His love for them in the different stages of childhood: crawling, talking, toddling, piggyback rides! (Then, of course, came the teenage years ... Just kidding.) God continued to show Himself to be the giver of the best gifts, indeed the only good gifts.

In the garden, humanity was set on the path of bondage, adopting a worldly human point of view. Blind spiritually and separated from the Lord, Adam and Eve were still pursued, protected, and influenced by the Father who made them and was committed to redeeming them from slavery to themselves. The darkness of their self-centeredness and the lies of the enemy brought into focus the light of God's love for them. This stood in stark contrast with the black deception of Satan's hatred for them, which was clear no matter how he dressed it up. Adam and Eve were made to see this that they might know the real light from the dark, life from death, and good from evil.

"Watch and pray, lest you enter into temptation. The spirit indeed is willing, but the flesh is weak" (Matt. 26:41). God has always intended to be our sole provider, and after the expulsion from the garden, He became our protector, helper, and provider, because we are exceedingly weak without His Spirit in us. Now, outside of the garden and our original union with God, the reality of the curse—that we must toil for what physically sustains us—was plain as we and all living things decayed and died.

THE KINGDOM OF HEAVEN

*E*VEN AS I TRY TO IMAGINE our life to come in the kingdom of heaven, I realize that I am fundamentally centered on my own. However, the Holy Spirit can change our point of view and our imaginative powers. Imagining a sinless existence is not possible for anyone this side of physical death, but the Spirit helps those imaginations that find God moment to moment by focusing on things above.

Far above all else, Jesus will provide everything that our life requires and will complete all of our desires. We will need absolutely nothing more. Praise God because while He has saved us from death, He has not stopped there and has made us children in the divine family with all its resources and privileges. He will give us life that can never be anything but everlasting, will bestow perfect mental, emotional, physical, and spiritual health, and will give us natural heavenly harmony with all people and a joy that never ends.

Best of all, we will have Jesus to see, to touch, to converse with, to look right in the eye, and to love in person, and this will be a love of wondrous bliss such as we have never experienced on earth.

There is a desire of the Spirit living in many believers to have the biggest possible multitude of worshipers in heaven. Worship, praise, and prayer down here are so much better in all ways with more souls involved together. In heaven, this experience will be even better, and while I acknowledge that it is selfish to want to enjoy this with as many souls as can be there, the Lord knows my point of view will change up there.

"And I heard a loud voice from heaven saying, 'Behold, the tabernacle of God is with men, and He will dwell with them, and they shall be His people. God Himself will be with them and be their God. And God will wipe away every tear from their eyes; there shall be no more death, nor sorrow, nor crying. There shall be no more pain, for the former things have passed away.' Then He who sat on the throne said, 'Behold, I make all things new'" (Rev. 21:3–5).

In the New King James Version of the Bible, our Lord uses the phrase "the kingdom of heaven is like" at least eleven times when graciously teaching spiritual truths. To be sure, the Holy Spirit translates these human- language teachings into a heavenly language that our body, soul, and spirit can understand and can actually feed on as we would feed on food. Food is broken down and converted into compounds that the body needs to grow. Likewise, the Holy Spirit causes our spirit to incorporate Bible doctrine in a divine process that rebuilds our heart of faith and grafts in Jesus' power to believe, producing growth and visible new life. What once was dead is now reborn; the dried-up shriveled seed sprouts up and grows in word and deed to maturity from the nutrients and water of the Word of God.

Without the Holy Spirit, any message about the kingdom of heaven will not be received in spirit and in truth. A sanctified imagination is needed to believe, to meditate on, and place solid hope in the reality that "surely the kingdom of God has come upon you" (Luke 11:20).

What does life in the coming kingdom look like, and how shall we live there?

The most important part of the coming kingdom is described in Revelation 4, Ezekiel 1–3, and Isaiah 6. The throne of God and all those in His presence, the worship, and the alien majesty and glory of that scene indicate that this is the center of our existence, the place and purpose for which we were created. When the saints are there, with God in their immediate presence, all things are whole and as right as God is right, holy, and good. Any other notions of what we will do and how we shall live will be revealed then and there, but I can't help believing that His throne will be where everyone will want to be.

"In My Father's house are many mansions; if it were not so, I would have told you. I go to prepare a place for you. And if I go and prepare a place for you, I will come again and receive you to Myself; that where I am, there you may be also" (John 14:2–3). Apparently, we will have housing of some sort (the best we have ever had, seeing as how Jesus prepared it for us) and it will be associated with the

Father's dwelling place. Is this a location? Will it even be a house as we think of one?

The English word *mansion* was derived from a Latin word, *mansum,* which means *to dwell. Mansion* in the King James Version of the Bible is translated from the original Greek word *mone,* pronounced *moh-nay,* which means *to stay,* or *to reside.* Solomon prayed to the Lord at the consecration and opening of the first temple in Jerusalem, God's chosen dwelling place on earth, "Behold, heaven and the heaven of heavens cannot contain You ... hear [us] from heaven Your dwelling place" (2 Chron. 6:18, 33).

This raises speculation that we will "dwell' and "stay' where God is— namely, the whole universe. Now there's a thought!

Comprehension of the kingdom of heaven is as possible (or impossible) as comprehension of God Himself. For example, the Bible has this to say:

> *Now I saw a new heaven and a new earth, for the first heaven and the first earth had passed away. Also there was no more sea ... the holy city, New Jerusalem, coming down out of heaven from God, prepared as a bride adorned for her husband ... having the glory of God. Her light was like a most precious stone, like a jasper stone, clear as crystal. Also she had a great and high wall with twelve gates, and twelve angels at the gates, and names written on them, which are the names of the twelve tribes of the children of Israel: three gates on the east, three gates on the north, three gates on the south, and three gates on the west. Now the*

wall of the city had twelve foundations, and on them were the names of the twelve apostles of the Lamb.

The city is laid out as a square; its length is as great as its breadth. And he measured the city with the reed: twelve thousand furlongs. Its length, breadth, and height are equal. Then he measured its wall: one hundred and forty-four cubits, according to the measure of a man, that is, of an angel. The construction of its wall was of jasper; and the city was pure gold, like clear glass. The foundations of the wall of the city were adorned with all kinds of precious stones: the first foundation was jasper, the second sapphire, the third chalcedony, the fourth emerald, the fifth sardonyx, the sixth sardius, the seventh chrysolite, the eighth beryl, the ninth topaz, the tenth chrysoprase, the eleventh jacinth, and the twelfth amethyst. The twelve gates were twelve pearls: each individual gate was of one pearl. And the street of the city was pure gold, like transparent glass.

—Rev. 21:1, 2, 10–14, 17–21

New Jerusalem is probably a cube; its length, height, and width are equal. The size of New Jerusalem is enormous; twelve thousand furlongs equals fifteen hundred miles. Bible scholar David Guzik notes that this is the distance from Maine to Florida and that the square footage would approximate the size of the moon.

Impressive is not the word. Yes, human language does its inadequate best to speak about a reality so huge, perfect, and gloriously beautiful that it is as out of reach as a whole other dimension. However, the fact that heaven is described at all is significant, considering that Scripture up to that point reveals little about it, certainly not to the degree in Revelation. "But as it is written: 'Eye has not seen, nor ear heard, nor have entered into the heart of man the things which God has prepared for those who love Him'" (1 Cor. 2:9). "He was caught up into Paradise and heard inexpressible words, which it is not lawful for a man to utter" (2 Cor. 12:4).

As staggering as heaven's description is, its Creator is far more than that.

> *But I saw no temple in it, for the Lord God Almighty and the Lamb are its temple. The city had no need of the sun or of the moon to shine in it, for the glory of God illuminated it. The Lamb is its light … Its gates shall not be shut at all by day (there shall be no night there) … And he showed me a pure river of water of life, clear as crystal, proceeding from the throne of God and of the Lamb. In the middle of its street, and on either side of the river, was the tree of life, which bore twelve fruits, each tree yielding its fruit every month. The leaves of the tree were for the healing of the nations … There shall be no night there: They need no lamp nor light of the sun, for the Lord God gives them light.*

> —*Rev. 21:22–23, 25; 22:1–2, 5*

This is where all human existence is supposed to lead us. It is wondrous that the Lord of the universe gave Himself for us. It is equally wondrous that we can't see ourselves for what we really are and what we've done. We are beloved children fallen into virtual helplessness because of our sins, but without Him we cannot know this or even hope to make it to where everlasting life in heaven awaits! He loves us and gave His all to get us there.

His love, manifested in our delivery to perfect reality, is how "in Him all things consist" (Col. 1:17). The coming kingdom is not at all like the place where we are now, even though when He was on earth the Lord prayed, "Your kingdom come. Your will be done on earth as it is in heaven" (Matt. 6:10).

The essence of perfect completion will be the full, unveiled, physical presence of God with men. The truth is, "No one has seen God at any time" (John 4:12). We will see and touch Him. "We know that when He is revealed, we shall be like Him, for we shall see Him as He is" (1 John 3:2).

We will not be saved as comforted refugees but as His children, and His love will be written on us.

"Behold, the tabernacle of God is with men, and He will dwell with them, and they shall be His people. God Himself will be with them and be their God. And God will wipe away every tear from their eyes; there shall be no more death, nor sorrow, nor crying. There shall be no more pain, for the former things have passed away" (Rev. 21:3–4).

"He said to me, 'It is done! I am the Alpha and the Omega, the Beginning and the End. I will give of the fountain of the water of life freely to him who thirsts. He who overcomes shall inherit all things, and I will be his God and he shall be My son'" (Rev. 21:6–7).

"And there shall be no more curse, but the throne of God and of the Lamb shall be in it, and His servants shall serve Him. They shall see His face, and His name shall be on their foreheads" (Rev. 22:3-4).

"He who sat on the throne said, 'Behold, I make all things new'" (Rev. 21:50).

The One at the center of our hearts' desires and dreams will actually be there with us! Yes! Besides the fact that "we shall be like Him," the blessed of the Lord will live very differently than they did in this mortal world.

"He who overcomes shall be clothed in white garments; I will confess his name before My Father and before His angels" (Rev. 3:5).

"To him who overcomes I will give to eat from the tree of life, which is in the midst of the Paradise of God" (Rev. 2:7).

"To him who overcomes I will give some of the hidden manna to eat. And I will give him a white stone, and on the stone a new name written which no one knows except him who receives it" (Rev. 2:17).

"And he who overcomes, and keeps My works until the end, to him I will give power over the nations, and I will give him the morning star" (Rev. 2:26–27).

"He who overcomes, I will make him a pillar in the temple of My God, and he shall go out no more. I will write on him the name of My God and the name of the city of My God, the New Jerusalem, which comes down out of heaven from My God. And I will write on him My new name" (Rev. 3:12).

"To him who overcomes I will grant to sit with Me on My throne, as I also overcame and sat down with My Father on His throne" (Rev. 3:21).

The causes and effects of the sin of Adam and all men after will be all that heaven is *not*. Heaven will be what all human beings yearn for, whether they believe in Jesus or not. He will make heaven happen when He makes all things new. The incomparable part of the coming kingdom will be the gift of the morning star; Jesus Himself, in all His glory!

Loretta Lynn sings a popular country song titled "Everybody Wants to Go to Heaven (but Nobody Wants to Die)." Do you want to go to heaven before death? Do you believe that "the God and Father of our Lord Jesus Christ ... has blessed us with every spiritual blessing in the heavenly places in Christ" (Eph 1:3)? Then depend on God in all things at all times, in all places. We will do this in heaven, removed from sin and free from the attachments of life that we so casually embrace here. God is love and light—holy, good, just, pure, generous, eternal, and perfect. The kingdom of heaven and its citizens will be that way, and not like us now on the earth we ravage.

Charles H. Spurgeon wrote of the kingdom of heaven with a vast wonder about our future.

In the sure future the better world will have inhabitants that don't rely on having a particular comfort level. Clothing will not wear out or become dirty and they will be free of style or concern for appearance. Medicine will be of the last world and unnecessary because not one will even feel sick. Praising God in the heavenly temple will take the place of sleep or daily rest as they will not need the restoration they require from it here and now. Jesus will fill their hearts so full with a desire for His presence that the dependence they have now for social life will not be essential to the bliss they experience.

The citizens of heaven will still be blessed with the ability to grow and learn, but they will all be taught from the perfect source of perfect knowledge and experience by the perfect Teacher, the Lord Himself. They receive provision from God for their sustenance and use here, but there they will be served a feast at the King's table. Here they receive help from the men the Lord sends and uses for their comfort, but there they will lean on the Beloved Lord Himself and Him alone. All their needs will be met by Christ Jesus Himself, and His provision never will be lost, taken, or fade. If they are working for their supply of water here, there is an eternally free-flowing open source of actual living water from the Fountain Himself, God in person.

The angels will no longer be the messengers of God's blessings and love letters to them because they will see Him face-to-face in love, in person. How tremendous to pass from beyond this world's separation from Jesus to enter into the actual embrace of the Savior feeling his glorious body holding our glorious body! How marvelous it will be to have God Himself and not His creation or His works as our constant joy! Their souls will then have attained the perfection of bliss.

THE FALL TO THE
SECOND ADVENT

W HEN THE FIRST HUMANS BECAME DISTORTED, no longer God-centered but self-centered, they were separated from God and from each other. This separation is as intense, real, and dramatically tragic as the difference between our world and heaven.

There have been so many attempts to show the horrible incompatibility of our sinfulness with God's perfect holiness, but I can find none that pictures it with enough clarity. If we could easily see the great chasm between fallen man and the holiness of God, we might not struggle so mightily with the attachments of this world.

Any separation from our Savior caused by attachment to ourselves and material things in preference to Him can prompt us to compare the high calling of God in Christ to our earthly need, or more truly, our earthly "want."

The Bible is replete with passages about men finding themselves suddenly in the presence of God and being struck down as if they are dead or blinded by the glory of His image. Fear for their lives reduces them to a trembling mass. Saul of Tarsus found himself sightless and without strength on the road to Damascus. The prophet Daniel was so devastated by the holy presence that he had to be touched by the One from heaven three times just to stand upright and be able to comprehend or speak. Peter, James, and John fell on their faces and were greatly afraid at the transfiguration of Christ and the cloud from which the Father spoke.

Were Adam and Eve like that? There is no indication in Scripture that when the Lord walked with them in the garden they were afflicted as the sinners Saul and Daniel (or others) were. In heaven, we will not be paralyzed by the fear our current state would produce in God's physical presence. Why? We are made holy by faith in Christ and cleansed by confession of our sins, so we can embrace the Lord with nothing of this world in our hearts, only Him. Soon this short trip will be over. Let us live now like we are already in the heavenly places being blessed by what is invisible to us now but what will be beautifully visible then.

"Has then what is good become death to me? Certainly not! But sin, that it might appear sin, was producing death in me through what is good, so that sin through the commandment might become exceedingly sinful" (Rom. 7:13).

The harsh, wrenching reality that the innocent Son of God would have to be so viciously treated and willingly endures the worst death possible for our atonement makes clear our utter inability to repair our separation from God with our filthy, sinful efforts.

With the multiplication of humans over time, the separation still existed but became more complicated with more self-absorbed "units." Added to this, people had to work for a living. Adam and Eve were not supposed to sit around eating bon-bons all day before the fall, but their activity was God-centered, done out of pure love for Him. They did not view their activity in life as a means of survival and their work as toil.

New difficulties added to their uphill battle after the fall. "Cursed is the ground for your sake; in toil you shall eat of it all the days of your life. Both thorns and thistles it shall bring forth for you, and you shall eat the herb of the field. In the sweat of your face you shall eat bread till you return to the ground, for out of it you were taken; for dust you are, and to dust you shall return" (Gen. 3:17–19).

There is no reason to suppose that before the fall humans were gatherers only, but the fact that they now had to sweat to extract food from a cursed land full of weeds points to the toil of cultivation. Gone is the sense of food as a joyous part of God's peaceful gift to life before these awful events.

Our God is so very, very gracious to us! He offered men a glimpse of what the removal of the curse of thorns and thistles would be like when He gave them manna from heaven and water out of the rock at Meribah, promised the Sabbath-year provision, and multiplied fish and bread in the hands of His Son Jesus. He spoke through Moses: "And of Joseph he said: 'Blessed of the Lord is his land, with the precious things of heaven, with the dew, and the deep lying beneath, with the precious fruits of the sun, with the precious produce of the months, with the best things of the ancient mountains, with the precious things of the everlasting hills, with the precious things of the earth and its fullness, and the favor of Him who dwelt in the bush. Let the blessing come'" (Deut. 33:13–16).

He also spoke through Amos.

> *"Behold, the days are coming," says the Lord, "when the plowman shall overtake the reaper, and the treader of grapes him who sows seed; the mountains shall drip with sweet wine, and all the hills shall flow with it. I will bring back the captives of My people Israel; they shall build the waste cities and inhabit them; they shall plant vineyards and drink wine from them; they shall also make gardens and eat fruit from them. I will plant them in their land, and no longer shall they be pulled up from the land I have given them," says the Lord your God.*
>
> *—Amos 9:13–15*

At the exit from Eden, God was not happy with Adam and Eve. He was righteously angry at that time of judgment. However, "His anger is but for a moment, His favor is for life; weeping may endure for a night, but joy comes in the morning" (Ps. 30:5).

To say that the Lord's righteousness, mercy, and purity are comforting and encouraging is the greatest understatement of all, especially for beginners in the life to which many of us have grown accustomed. We have been taught to believe that God Almighty is always here, there, and everywhere. He most certainly was close to those first selfish people, who must have been overwhelmed with themselves, with fear, guilt, and most of all, separation from their Father. But in this state they were about to find out just how strong and unchanging is our Lord's tender, loving kindness!

We have not known the bonding and unifying Spirit of God in a large population such as the one that could have existed in Eden and will exist in heaven. Why can't we all just get along?

Our inability to love and relate to other humans and treasure God's creation through the One we worship brought into being the sad notion of "man-made." At this stage of man's post-garden history, people changed into individuals driven above all else by their perceived individual needs even while being compelled to relate to and be with others, just as God made us to do. This was a problem, maybe the first and biggest problem God needed to help men overcome. The Lord had not abandoned them and settled for a second-best scenario with humans. He controlled the transition perfectly and intimately as a father raises children.

Choice is the most wonderful and most terrible aspect of our makeup. What was it like not even to consider looking to ourselves instead of looking to God? It seems that we looked only to God before the serpent deceived our parents. With the plan of redemption now in effect, choosing to reconnect with the Lord is indisputably the right choice. But we don't always do that, and neither did our ancestors right out of the garden. Nonetheless, God was still beautiful in all that He made and provided for the first family. He still beckoned.

It is not known what survival and toil was like back at the beginning, but eventually, with a larger population, people felt a greater need to toil together in peace to provide efficient prosperity. The need must have made clear either directly through God or by circumstance. Over time, this need for compatibility in work and life in general has only grown, and become important in many more dimensions.

Enter man-made organization. Why? Our Lord always requires that we choose to be guided in all aspects of life by Him. Sin has ruined us, and we have defaulted to the new guidance system: ourselves. Was what we call a "learning curve" an ancient experience, too? Perhaps so, and the pioneers in a newly godless society must have trashed things pretty badly given their inexperience—especially with the help of the fallen angels.

THE WICKEDNESS AND JUDGMENT OF MAN

*N*ow it came to pass, when men began to multiply on the face of the earth, and daughters were born to them, that the sons of God saw the daughters of men, that they were beautiful; and they took wives for themselves of all whom they chose. And the Lord said, 'My Spirit shall not strive with man forever, for he is indeed flesh; yet his days shall be one hundred and twenty years.'

There were giants on the earth in those days, and also afterward, when the sons of God came in to the daughters of men and they bore children to them. Those were the mighty men who were of old, men of renown. Then the Lord saw that the wickedness of man was great in the earth, and that every intent of the thoughts of his heart was only evil continually. And the Lord was sorry that He had made man on the earth, and He was grieved in His heart. So the Lord said, 'I will destroy man whom I have created from the face of the earth, both man and beast, creeping thing and birds of the air, for I am sorry that I have made them.' But Noah found grace in the eyes of the Lord.

—Gen. 6:1–7

What a distorted scene. Not only were self-willed humans pushing the limits of a civilized peace, but the enemy of God had his troops raping the female population, producing offspring that were perversions of nature and polluting the human gene pool. This sounds like a big problem. But the most horrific reality of those times was that "The earth also was corrupt before God, and the earth was filled with violence. So God looked upon the earth, and indeed it was corrupt; for all flesh had corrupted their way on the earth" (Gen. 6:11–12).

When I was twelve, I spent a few hours completely convinced that a nuclear war would happen at any minute. I looked to the sky and expected a huge flash with every beat of my heart. The whole earth was going to be destroyed, and I would be destroyed with it. "The earth also was corrupt … the earth was filled with violence."

A deep grief over the destruction of everything we hold dear is an experience many have had, and God's grief must have been God-size. How could this be? How could we have done this to Him? How could we not?

As Genesis 6 tells us, there were many crossbreeds in the population, and these mighty human-angel beings also greatly contributed to the increasing corruption and violence on the earth. The woman's seed, Christ Himself, might never have been a pure human, and thus humanity's redemption could not have taken place. However, God is never unprepared.

"Noah found grace in the eyes of the Lord" (Gen. 6:8). If there was any improvement in the organization of self-centered men living and working together, it was taken aboard the ark with Noah and his family. Selfish behavior taken to its worst extreme was nearly wiped out from the face of the earth. Noah and his family still had the nature of their ancestors, all the way back to Adam.

Because people are so inwardly oriented, the development of a stronger and stronger attachment to personal needs led to problems that put humans at odds with each other. We can only wonder what the first serious disagreement was like and how it turned out. Did it get solved to the satisfaction of both parties? Did they fail to get anywhere and give up? Did disagreement lead to violence?

"Cain was very angry, and his countenance fell. So the Lord said to Cain, 'Why are you angry? And why has your countenance fallen? If you do well, will you not be accepted? And if you do not do well, sin lies at the door. And its desire is for you, but you should rule over it.' Now Cain talked with Abel his brother; and it came to pass, when they were in the field, that Cain rose up against Abel his brother and killed him" (Gen. 4:5–8).

God made us to be with each other and followed through with even more love than He showed in the creation. Human problems have been solved cooperatively, even unselfishly, even sacrificially. The Lord has taught us through experience and directly.

Larger populations must have required recognition of this cooperative existence between groups, best expressed through divine guidance. Separation of groups of people according to location, ability, age, willingness, and many other considerations in terms of survival needs made cooperation and organization necessary.

Different methods of getting food, clothing, and shelter came into being, and according to the individual capabilities of the people toiling for these things, the results came out differently. Comparing talents, acquisitions, and even geographical locations must have led some people to view themselves or others as having more or less success or anything else covetable. This was a recipe for ever-stronger attachments to individual needs and desires, creating further separation between individuals and groups based on self-image. Evaluation of people and their possessions increased.

However, we managed to get along well enough to obtain food, store it, and distribute it, process it, cook it, and develop tools and systems to do this and other essentials for ourselves and others. For all this to work, there had to be planning, communication, development of skills, projection of quantities, judgment, evaluation, and improvement. But long before this the family unit came into being, with the power of the Creator at its center.

Aspects of family relations are unique through divine purpose. To "be partakers of the divine nature" (2 Pet. 1:4) in its fullness within the family was a necessity. There was no Scripture offering familial instruction from God to the first family, but the Lord has since provided it.

Did the Lord instruct the first man and woman as to the hierarchy or "chain of command" in the first family, or were they to learn it as they went along? The situation sounds tragically like the one facing so many families today. After the first sin, nature took over; parenting by the seat of our pants, we trained our children in the same inadequate and unholy method from one generation to the next.

This seems especially out of place considering the descriptions of God's intimate, in-person existence with Adam and Eve in the garden and the revelation of our new nature in the kingdom of heaven. The essence of our sinful nature is that we instinctively put ourselves above all else, including our Creator. Why would we have to be told to do only what the Spirit of God leads us to do? With a sinful nature not yet afflicting our first parents, it would seem that they and the Spirit were in accord in every way. They would have been our instruction; now we are being transformed into God's will through sanctification by His Spirit.

The Lord has not abandoned any human who has lived. He is there, in love with each of us, responding to the seeker and intervening that we may turn to Him. He has instructed, and it is probable that He gave instruction to the first family. Ephesians 5:22–28 presents the bedrock of the husband-and-wife relationship; that bedrock is the Spirit of Jesus Christ. Colossians 3:18–22 extends that instruction to include the children's place in the family and holy submission to love between members as the rule in the family.

In his first epistle, chapter 3:1–9, Peter calls attention to the leading roles in the family, husband and wife. This section ends with a connection to the body of Christ and the world outside the family. Long before Peter and Paul and even the incarnate Christ, the first family grew to become a community and then more communities.

Intrafamilial relations, standards for living with others, and inclusion or exclusion of God in life have been passed on to the world at large up to this day. Material acquisitions, tied to insecurity about self-image, and all the damaging fallout (obsession with wealth, perceived power, and protection) have created the worst separation since the flood. The family became the world community, and now the family seems to be enslaved to conformity to that community. God's instruction must rule and eventually will.

Religion: a cause, principle, or system of beliefs held to with ardor and faith; the service and worship of God or the supernatural; a personal set or institutionalized system of religious attitudes, beliefs, and practices.

A saint whose life the Holy Spirit has used to minister to me said that definitions from the dictionary are not a reliable or accurate source for biblical teaching, but I use this definition anyway to discuss the beginning of what we now call religion. The Lord's instruction to the first humans concerning family structure may have occurred in the garden, and He may also have taught them or led them to the worship of God. We were made in His image. "He has made everything beautiful in its time. Also He has put eternity in their hearts" (Eccl. 3:11).

How and when God began the teaching and guidance of humans in a right worshiping relationship with Him and in Him is not clearly detailed in Scripture, but such instruction was certainly necessary when we fell away from Him, expelled from paradise. The

Lord has been close and personal with man from the beginning, and it is likely that when He started the process of redemption He was just as accessible as He is now, maybe even more so.

It seems that correct worship in spirit and truth would have begun in the family. Just as life within the family had moved beyond the family to other families, the worship of God would have moved with it. The chances of this original worship and teaching from the Lord being changed from group to group and generation to generation must have been significant because of man's inexperience with the damage inflicted by his new selfish nature; he never even thought about it.

The enemy of God continued to influence the minds and flesh of people, just as he does today. So, looking at this ingredient, our new self-made image, our new self-centered imaginings, and our increasing distance over time from the beloved Creator, man-made religion was born, with the worship of someone or something else besides the one true God.

When did this happen? The Bible doesn't always focus on time frames, and the expanse of time from the fall to the flood is not clearly revealed. One thing seems sure. "The earth also was corrupt before God, and the earth was filled with violence. So God looked upon the earth, and indeed it was corrupt; for all flesh had corrupted their way on the earth." Therefore the worship of the perfect God, in obedience out of love for Him, did not become the central focus and unity of men on earth.

Did the structure of corporate worship and its hierarchy develop, disintegrate, and then rebound within the family, even before it reached the community level? History shows that religion has suffered from this internal struggle from ancient times to now. But the Lord knew this, and still the worship of God in a society of "self" has been a most necessary component of visible redemption in the world.

In the garden, we heard the command "Be fruitful and multiply; fill the earth and subdue it." We have done that, and we can't seem to escape doing it, but what on earth would humanity look like if we truly were all one in the Lord? Not in this life will we see that. No matter how well or badly humans got along, the earth became so filled with us that "civilizing" humanity, especially after the flood, became a matter of survival before we could yield any semblance of peace or prosperity. There will always be an undercurrent of yearning and separation in any state of human peace or prosperity this side of heaven.

Surely, there has been relative peace and relatively cooperative growth in all millennia throughout the globe since the fall. People somehow recognized the need to help each other, plan together, relate in some harmony as individuals and communities of all sizes, cultures, and locations, and pool resources for this relative common good, today and for the future. Amazing, considering the incomprehensibly violent anarchy of the pre-flood period. The Creator of the universe has done well with those He created with the ability to choose.

Too often, we take choice for granted, and indeed we consider it our right rather than a gift. But God has controlled the outcome of all our choices, whether we like it or not and whether we acknowledge it or not. The plan of redemption is going just as He wills. Whether we wield our will as a weapon for ourselves or as a mirror of Him in this world and the one to come, He loves us and has allowed us to get this far; though we are unspeakably enormous and hopelessly complex as a big family trying to make it without Dad.

In God's plan for redeeming us from ourselves He has given us a bit of the divine nature, even if we have gone bad. To create order out of chaos in populations of all sizes, He has chosen human authorities for their positions. We grew to huge proportions from our tiny beginning, and to accommodate our basic disunity, the order necessary for large populations rightly involves some form of governing (directing, controlling, strongly influencing), enforcement of that governing, and protection of that governing for the continuance of order. The governing body must itself be orderly and, one hopes, responsive to the population it governs. Planning, review, correction, prevention, and reorganization all come with the territory, at least in some populations.

Would all this incredibly wild organizational "order" we see now even be necessary if we loved the Lord our God with all we are and truly loved others as we loved ourselves? Maybe not. There will be order in the life to come, but not in the spirit by which we have maintained it so far.

SQUIRMING IN HIS HANDS

B LESSED IS OUR FATHER WHO ALWAYS gives us good things, no matter how we view them or use them. The wondrous world we live in is so tremendously beautiful and good. The Lord God Himself rested and commanded us to do the same. In this rest, we can come to know Him better, but we have not been able to focus our attention and our hearts on Him to any degree worth mentioning.

As it is written: "There is none righteous, no, not one; there is none who understands; there is none who seeks after God. They have all turned aside; they have together become unprofitable; there is none who does good, no, not one. Their throat is an open tomb; with their tongues they have practiced deceit; the poison of asps is under their lips, whose mouth is full of cursing and bitterness. Their feet are swift to shed blood; destruction and misery are in their ways; and the way of peace they have not known. There is no fear of God before their eyes."

—Rom. 3:10–18

With our roving hearts and minds, we have looked outside of ourselves and found a part of us that creates from the bit of divine ability the Lord gave us. Musical, literary, and artistic expressions have been the best things we have created for our benefit, and the best of all have been those that glorify our God. These are a very distant second best to worshiping God and seeking personal, divine, intimate knowledge of the Almighty, but they are amazing, especially when they point away from sin.

The drawback, of course, is in us. We have turned many of these creative expressions into magnifiers of our sinful nature, and even usurped the Lord's rightful place in our existence by worshiping these gifts. So many people look at and listen to what man has made and see more and more of man rather than God, who keeps the man.

Another wonderful gift from above is each of our brains, our intellect. Seeking, reasoning, deducting, hypothesizing, experimenting, communicating, exploring, and using logic are just a part of the incredible gift from God of our minds. When this gift is oriented correctly to the Lord, it leads to the foremost of Gods gifts to us, and that is belief. Faith empowers our minds to cooperate in the repair that He works in the world through our belief in Him, and thereby through our visible lives as everlasting beings. The sciences and philosophies of men are the result of our relatively amazing minds allowing us to do the best we can as fallen sinners. I say "relatively amazing" in comparison with the mind of Christ.

God has used every person throughout history to further His unchangeable plan for redeeming "whosoever will." Sure, men have taken everything God has given them as a gift to be used for His glory and have turned it into self-worship in varying degrees, but those who have "know[n] whom [they] have believed" (2 Tim. 1:12) also know the beginning of men on earth and, more important, they know the end of the earth (and mankind) as we know it.

What have we done with our gifts? We have certainly taken our God-given gift for science, especially in the technological realm, and have made the fastest and most powerful ride ever imagined so far. The lifetimes of the newest things are vaporous; they are quickly left behind, dismissed as too old by the time most of us first hear of them. In delightful contrast, our Redeemer says, "For I am the Lord, I do not change" (Mal. 3:6).

Religious author A. W. Tozer writes:

> *That God is immutable is not the most difficult thing to understand of all that we attempt to comprehend about Him. However, to really grasp it we must sort the thoughts we usually have concerning created things from the more rarified thoughts. The writers of scripture, possessing real spiritual health, looked squarely at man's mutability and wrote words of wholesome strength for us. They say that God changes not, and this is the remedy for our great illness. This fallen world changes, but God changes not. The change which the children of God experience through*

the indwelling Holy Spirit works for them and not against them. Living in a falling world of change and deterioration, even faithful people come short of complete happiness. From deep inside saints are drawn to that which does not change and feel mourning for the passing of dear familiar things.

God uses "modern" things and the people who make them and use them, even those who seem so ungodly, to get us all where He has determined we will be, keeping the ones who come along with Him and leaving the ones who will not. He remakes everything and is not diverted or slowed down one micron from what He wills, when He wills it. And a good will it is indeed!

So many good things have come from scientific minds for the benefit of us sinners dying from sin's decay. They are temporary benefits, but "who has despised the day of small things" (Zech. 4:10)? Jesus' everlasting benefits turn decay into regeneration. So many life-altering words have come to bear on humanity from the philosophical minds of history, and permanent, heavenly alterations have come from philosophers who are believers in the one true living God.

"Hear, O Israel: the Lord our God, the Lord is one!" (Deut. 6:4). "I, even I, am the Lord, and besides Me there is no savior" (Isa. 43:11).

To put it all in proper perspective, the Lord has indisputably used whomever He has chosen, believing or unbelieving, cooperative or reluctant. We think that we can do as God can and be as God is— that is, be in control. Our history has proved this. We are terribly out of place in this role, and we have been helpless at making the world better, let alone making our own individual lives right. No matter how hard we try, our relapse into sinful ways has been inevitable.

"CHECK IT OUT!"

A DVANCEMENT IS A WORTHY GOAL FOR mankind, but advancing to what, to where, by what means, and by whose authority? Those questions have always been the subject of hot debate. Without a doubt, "advancement" occurs in a seemingly mind-of-its-own way. It is not total anarchy and chaos, but self-centered beings have difficulty remaining focused on a common goal that does not also benefit themselves and their own.

Seems natural and logical, doesn't it? *Will my people and I get anything from attaining this goal?* By itself, this question and its motivation are not wrong. However, definitions of "taking care of ourselves and our own" vary wildly. When the extras or luxuries of life are deemed necessities, and gifts and privileges are considered rights, strife and separation usually ensue. So what are luxuries and privileges? Compare a couple of "limits" from the Bible.

"And having food and clothing, with these we shall be content" (1 Tim 6:8). "And Jesus said to him, 'Foxes have holes and birds of the air have nests, but the Son of Man has nowhere to lay His head'" (Matt. 8:20).

Worldly enticements deprive us of contentment, and the light of the prince of this world replaces the light of Jesus' Word. We step into a path advertised as heading for the "bright" top, but it leads down, a long way down.

The harvest that came from the work of our hands used to be the joyous payday provided by the Lord. "You have put gladness in my heart, More than in the season that their grain and wine increased" (Ps. 4:7). What is it now? Today there is a whole lot of harvesting and threshing of other people along with the work of our hands. But the Bible says "that he who plows should plow in hope, and he who threshes in hope should be partaker of his hope" (1 Cor. 9:10).

It takes a divine viewpoint to see man as he really is, God as He has revealed Himself, and how the twain should meet.

Left to ourselves, we are driven by self-sufficiency, followed or combined with self-gratification, followed or combined with self-protection. But all the while, the need implanted in us by God is constantly telling us that we are made to have healthy relationships. How strange it is that humanity has simultaneously strived for personal and communal independence while stressing the necessity of sacrificial love for harmony among all men; the majority of people on this globe have never achieved the two goals. God thinks globally and wills globally.

At the very moment we truly believed in Christ and asked Him into our lives as master and savior, we began everlasting life. From a divine viewpoint, this life before physical death is a microscopic part of our existence. The believer's view is that the best by far is yet to come—on the other side of death or with Jesus' return. This world and its stuff cannot compare with that future.

Also, the things of modern, worldly life cannot pass from here to heaven, but the things done in faith in this world can precede us into heaven. A comparison of the two through the eyes of faith makes clear the value of one and the relative worthlessness of the other. So, if we can't get what we want in any lasting way here on earth, can we put aside our temporal needs in favor of eternal rewards, using generously what God gives us for the enrichment and lifting up of others? The Lord will take care of us.

What if we looked forward to the clothing and appearance that we will receive from the Lord in His kingdom more than we worried about what others think as we deplete our God-given resources now? What if we stopped fretting about retirement, realizing that there is no real retirement for the servant of Christ? Besides, the rest above all rests is up yonder, and we know this through and through.

Say we want to visit the Holy City, for example, but put it off in this life. This world's version will pale profoundly compared with what we see in glory on our first trip there. Postponing that trip means using more of our God-given resources to advance the gospel of life and do what our Father sent us to do. Why not forsake *now* for *then* in matters of flesh and blood?

If here and now we are working for the King of heaven, we should realize that the money we use won't be honored or recognized in any transactions we have when we go home from this world. Much like spending all our euros or pesos before returning to the United States, we can give our dollars to the needy for the gospel's sake before we go to paradise. Ultimately, what creature comfort can't be forsaken for the Lord's work here, which will precede us into heaven?

CHRIST'S EARTHLY REVELATION

J ESUS REVEALED HIMSELF TO HUMANITY WHEN he spoke as a
man and spoke through His apostles. The Book of Revelation
at the end of the Bible is also a part of this disclosure to man.
But while He was revealing the way, the truth, and the life, opening
the door to God the Father through Himself, and establishing His
church after His resurrection and ascension, Jesus taught extensively
about man's wretched condition. He did not constantly wag His
finger at us for our pitiful lives and dull hearts. Instead, He spoke
of all the ways that we can be saved from ourselves and of all those
things that keep us lost and enslaved. The Lord's deep and tender
love is clear in His words of rescue to those He created.

His words are also stern and unyielding as He reveals the truth about the radical difference between real life in Himself and what we conceive life to be. In John 3:12, the Lord says to Nicodemus and to us, "If I have told you earthly things and you do not believe, how will you believe if I tell you heavenly things?"

What earthly things? In the context of Jesus' exchange with Nicodemus, earthly things are that which is born of the flesh, in contrast with that which is born of the spirit. In earthly terms, the wind is invisible and seems completely random even though we can feel it and hear it. Similarly, though we can't see the Spirit, we can feel Him in our lives and see the effects of rebirth in others. The Lord with patience then asks, "How will you believe if I tell you heavenly things?"

He tells us that we have everlasting life, that we shall not die, and that He will come and receive us to Himself so that where He is we also may be. So why do we seem to cling to the life down here and live as if this won't happen? He tells us through His apostle, "You died, and your life is hidden with Christ in God" (Col. 3:3). So why do we act before others as if it's *our* life?

He tells us to "seek the kingdom of God, and all these things shall be added to you" (Luke 12:31), then follows that with the difficult instruction to "Sell what you have and give alms; provide yourselves money bags which do not grow old" (Luke 12:33) and says to "lay up for yourselves treasures in heaven, where neither moth nor rust destroys and where thieves do not break in and steal" (Matt. 6:19-20). So why do we hold back and not believe Him?

Our resistance is especially foolish after Jesus tells us that it is He "who is able to do exceedingly abundantly above all that we ask or think" (Eph. 3:20) and "my God shall supply all your need according to His riches in glory by Christ Jesus" (Phil. 4:19). And: "Give, and it will be given to you: good measure, pressed down, shaken together, and running over will be put into your bosom. For with the same measure that you use, it will be measured back to you" (Luke 6:38).

We tell ourselves that we believe this and will do what the Lord has asked of us when He asks us, right? But do we want to know what we really believe? Look at how we behave, how we live. What is God's? What is ours? "For where your treasure is, there your heart will be also" (Luke 12:34).

Above all else, the Lord proclaimed the truth that He is the Creator, rightful ruler, and God of all our lives and the whole universe. Calling on Him is a huge leap of faith, especially for those who see the end of their self-rule as the end of their existence. But most amazing of all, He says all this and does not demand faith, submission, and obedience from those He has made and continues to give physical life to. He doesn't even demand that of those to whom He gives everlasting spiritual life.

Author J. P. Moreland says, "God maintains a delicate balance between keeping His existence sufficiently evident so people know He's there, and yet hiding His presence enough so that people who want to choose to ignore Him can do it. This way, their choice of [eternal] destiny is really free."

"Now great multitudes went with Him. And He turned and said to them, 'If anyone comes to Me and does not hate his father and mother, wife and children, brothers and sisters, yes, and his own life also, he cannot be My disciple. And whoever does not bear his cross and come after Me cannot be My disciple … whoever of you does not forsake all that he has cannot be My disciple. He who has ears to hear, let him hear!'" (Luke 14:25–27, 33, 35).

What disaster the wrong choice leads to, and what immense reward the right choice leads to! Yet for the right choice to bring an immense reward in the truest sense for the giver and the receiver, the receiver must be free to choose to accept eternal salvation and free to choose the life that requires. Humanity as a whole has not made the right choice, but that is not the perception of vast portions of mankind.

> *For God did not send His Son into the world to condemn the world, but that the world through Him might be saved. He who believes in Him is not condemned; but he who does not believe is condemned already, because he has not believed in the name of the only begotten Son of God. And this is the condemnation, that the light has come into the world, and men loved darkness rather than light, because their deeds were evil. For everyone practicing evil hates the light and does not come to the light, lest his deeds should be exposed. But he who does the truth comes to the light, that his deeds may be clearly seen, that they have been done in God.*

> *—John 3:17–21*

As persons, we think independently. This passage tells us that salvation is a matter of choosing and believing—believing Christ's words about salvation and condemnation; living in the light rather than in the darkness; doing deeds of truth and not deeds of evil; choosing to come out of our condemnation to our salvation in the Son of God.

But the Lord is also talking about whom we recognize as our ruler. Is it ourselves or Jesus? We tend to think independently about this passage; *we* will define the light and the dark for ourselves, thank you! *We* will decide whether our whole existence has been spent walled off inside our own personal fortress, thank you! Left to himself, man can't seem to help but choose the only one he's ever known well enough to be his ruler: himself.

Christ talked about darkness, and it is well known that when you want to be hidden or to hide something, darkness does the trick, or certainly is an advantage. Darkness hides things *from* us as well. The truth of the good ruler, the Good Shepherd, and the King has been hidden, and is being hidden from the people of this world by the same darkness they have actually chosen, even if they say they have not chosen it. How can we tell light from darkness when the prince of darkness has convinced us that his darkness is the light? It is not. We are deceived by the darkness in evaluating the worthiness of our self-rule.

"Then Jesus spoke to them again, saying, 'I am the light of the world. He who follows Me shall not walk in darkness, but have the light of life'" (John 8:12). "As long as I am in the world, I am the light of the world" (John 9:5).

When the Son of God opens a man's eyes, he can see the light from the dark and becomes part of the light by faith in the light of the world. "You are the light of the world. A city that is set on a hill cannot be hidden" (Matt. 5:14).

PLUCK IT OUT

"*A*ND HE SAID TO THEM, 'TAKE heed and beware of covetousness, for one's life does not consist in the abundance of the things he possesses'" (Luke 12:15). This verse is one that many people hold up as true and right, whether they are Christian or not. However, when people are put to the test in reality, especially quickly and by surprise, the truth can hurt badly, the rightness of it can seem unfair, and the covetousness is clear for all to see, especially in the one tested.

I have had everything changed, "taken," lost (or so it seemed) in a short time, and I remember wailing, "My life is ruined! It's over!" Not according to Christ. The beautiful creation still exists, and more important, so does the beautiful Creator. If we are bought as a possession by Jesus' blood, brought into the royal family of God, all that is His is ours, and Christ has never lost or ruined *anything*. Therefore, whatever happens to the things we "possess" in "our" lives is true, right, and fair when our hearts have been remade in Christ. Watch what you wish for because you reap what you sow.

We seem to have hands and arms coming out of our eyes and taking what we see—possession on sight. Have you ever learned about something that you previously never knew or cared about and been hit with the sudden urge to have it? Have you seen this in other people?

How shall the Word of God that enters us leave to accomplish its mission if we live like we haven't received it? How shall our light shine and glorify our Father in heaven if our hearts and minds first real concern is whether we are wearing the coolest designer sunglasses over the lamp of the soul? Will we see just how beautiful "the feet of those who preach the gospel of peace, who bring glad tidings of good things" (Isa. 52:7) really are if we fret about whether they are shod with expensive, name-brand shoes?

We grab what we covet with our eyes and pull it into the hiding place of our ravenous self-image, our self-preservation, our self-consciousness, a space that is never full. This hiding place is not intended for this or for us. The heart, like the rest of us, is made for God and is supposed to be a place where the Lord alone dwells. We are to clean our hearts repeatedly in repentant purity and, by our personal will to be made holy, make room for Him only—not for an abundance of coveted possessions, personal images, and selfish desires, with God in there somewhere.

The things we look at and let our hearts and minds linger upon become more than visual, intellectual, and emotional experiences that come and go; they leave an imprint. Those imprints can be a snare and a diversion for us unless we set our minds "on things above, not on things on the earth" (Col. 3:2). If we make it a holy habitual purpose to trust more and more that Jesus is king of all, aware and working good out of this entire weird world for "those who love God, to those who are the called according to His purpose" (Rom. 8:28), we can look at the things that may leave a harmful imprint on us and ensnare us and hand them to Him, just as we hand Him our sin; we leave it and go on unspotted from the world.

4-D Vision: Holy/Unholy, Valuable/Valueless

*T*HE LORD MADE THE DAY AS light and the night as dark. Jesus is the light of the world, and the enemy is the ruler of darkness. Salvation is of the Lord, and the wages of sin are death. As saints, we have both before us all the time in this world. The unbelieving see the darkness and think it's the light, or they seek the light where it does not exist. See and have joy in the Lord who is, by His spirit, everywhere in reality. Hallelujah!

It seems logical and natural to rely on the world as it is, moment to moment, for the purposes of living here. It seems clear that God intended His creation to be as perfect as He is, and if it were to change, it would be by His design and permission, by His control and His will. This has happened. We live in a changing world even if the Lord Himself is not changing. His Word tells us that we should not rely on the world but on the unchanging God as a secure foundation for our existence. He is going to shake this place.

"See that you do not refuse Him who speaks. For if they did not escape who refused Him who spoke on earth, much more shall we not escape if we turn away from Him who speaks from heaven, whose voice then shook the earth; but now He has promised, saying, 'Yet once more I shake not only the earth, but also heaven.' Now this, 'Yet once more,' indicates the removal of those things that are being shaken, as of things that are made, that the things which cannot be shaken may remain" (Heb. 12:25–27).

▽▲

The earth is built upon by men to reach higher than other men. The sure future is that many will be on top of small, medium, and huge heaps of stocks, smug in their self-images, personal conquests, and possessions, when the Changer of the universe will change everything. Will those who fall from the heights experience the Lord's merciful humbling on the way down and see that "Whoever falls on that stone will be broken; but on whomever it falls, it will grind him to powder" (Luke 20:8)?

Jesus' breaking can bring anyone down to the perfect place where He is the only one who can save and reassemble them with the purpose of making them into jewels in His crown at the very top. God is at once the builder and the wrecking ball. When people reach the top of the world, they discover in the end it is a long way down to the bottom. But Jesus is there also to take those willing to go with Him. "For such a High Priest was fitting for us, who is holy, harmless, undefiled, separate from sinners, and has become higher than the heavens" (Heb. 7:26).

We too are to be "holy, harmless, undefiled, separate from sinners" as servants of Christ in humility. We will be exalted in heaven by the Spirit sent from the King. We are to be in this world, but not of this world. We are here on assignment with a work visa from another world. We can determine what is valuable or valueless, good or evil, light or darkness, top or bottom by our orientation to the King of heaven, the place where we will go when the visa is expired. All that we have is in heaven, and we are not to build worthless heaps and hurt ourselves and our Lord by falling from them.

Some in this world of man-made self-image will not honor our Master, whose name is on our visa, or the work of salvation we do as helpers. They will confront us with direct conflict and worldly temptation to distract and disorient us, maybe even to destroy us. "But the multitude of the city was divided: part sided with the Jews, and part with the apostles. And when a violent attempt was made by both the Gentiles and Jews, with their rulers, to abuse and stone them, they became aware of it and fled to Lystra and Derbe, cities of Lycaonia, and to the surrounding region" (Acts 14:4–6).

For the inhabitants of this world who are not Christ's, the end, the bottom, of the long way to the top is death. Contemplating life's troubles, the unbelieving ask, "What's the worst thing that could happen? You could be dead, but you're not." For the child of God, death is where Christ the Door takes His own to the kingdom of heaven, beyond and above all that is here. Let us not allow attachment to this world, no matter how slick or indispensable it may look, to rule our hearts, the dwelling place of Jesus, our Lord and Savior. Let us not be dragged down by looking to the wrong top place.

$$\triangledown\blacktriangle$$

"Now godliness with contentment is great gain" (1 Tim. 6:6). Birth, school, work, death. This is a human view of life in chunks of extremely limited description. Though not all people hold this viewpoint, it seems to be the norm in many cultures. Yes, many people do not have as much education as others, or any at all. Work, made possible for most by physical health, is not possible, difficult, or very different for some. The Lord provides limitless variety in life. That variety is the work of God in us and through us.

"But Jesus answered them, 'My Father has been working until now, and I have been working'" John 5:17). Life is mostly hard work. The work our Lord assigned to the first humans in the garden was not hard toil. The work powered by the Holy Spirit in regenerated humans is not hard toil. It is the pleasure of "faith working through love" (Gal. 5:16). The holy, transforming work that Jesus accomplishes in us and with us is growing, gracious abundant life. It becomes hard toil only when we let it become so by failing to abide with the Lord. The early twentieth-century minister Oswald Chambers puts it this way:

> Sharpen the focus of your life onto your individual circumstances. Is your will so involved with the Lord's life that nothing much matters except that you are His child, always talking with Him and watching how all things come from His hands? Does the everlasting child within you live in

His house in His kingdom within you? Is His wondrous life-giving Spirit of grace ministering through you at your home, your work, and in your social life? Have you questioned why you are going through the things you are? Because of the unique way the Son of God has come in His Father's lordship into your life as a saint is the totality of why you go through anything. Let Him have his way and cling to His lordship to your core. The vitality of a simple life through Jesus comes just that way; through Jesus. The life He lived among us when He was here is the life He works and lives in us, in the midst of those around us.

Birth and death are shared by all. We perceive our history as the combined lives of all people in terms of this abbreviated birth-school-work-death description of human life. God has not made us to be limited by human description, and indeed, we have pushed the scope of everything between birth and death beyond limits, willfully changing these boundaries all the time. The spiritual dimension of life has been left far behind in the great expansion of our corporate and individual efforts throughout history. This explains the repeated reference to a "remnant" throughout the Bible.

Though our fallen state does not facilitate a pure life with God, we are assured of being a new creation in Christ, completely and utterly new in heaven, our sinful nature vanished. As Scripture says, "Eye has not seen, nor ear heard, nor have entered into the heart of man the things which God has prepared for those who love Him" (1 Cor. 2:9).

So how do we deal with the cumulative effects of man's viewpoint on this world we now live in? How should we perceive them in daily life? How much of our vision is human viewpoint? The heap we have created keeps growing! For us, the process may be irreversible, but the Lord will certainly have His time of re-creation.

However, we must still learn how to live holy lives in this world. All creation and real change come first from the heart—the heart of God renewing the hearts of men. Worldwide changes that have encompassed groups of people, then systems, then perhaps even our natural environment, have come from a change in men's hearts. We have seen this happen just as the kingdom of God swept over this messy world through the life, death, resurrection, and ascension of a single man, God made into flesh. Some have seen the path to change with divine vision, and some have seen it with human vision. God has made our hearts, and He wants to change them forever.

"Yet indeed I also count all things loss for the excellence of the knowledge of Christ Jesus my Lord, for whom I have suffered the loss of all things, and count them as rubbish, that I may gain Christ" (Phil. 3:8). How do we go from wondering how to live a holy life in this world to counting all things loss for the excellence of the knowledge of Christ? Jesus is the creator, sustainer, and goal of all existence. When we purpose our wills to abide in His presence, our viewpoint is changed to conform with our Lord's unalterable plan to save us and to place us as His holy witnesses. Though the dead, dying, perverse, and physical may feel like it is inescapable, it's blocking our vision, and rubbing all over us as we live here, we are holy and a living redeemed force in all of it.

This handwritten sign was reportedly found on the wall of Mother Teresa's room:

People are unreasonable, illogical, and self centered; forgive them anyway. If you are kind, people may accuse you of selfish, ulterior motives; be kind anyway. If you are successful, you will win some false friends, and some true enemies; be successful anyway. What you have spent years building, someone could destroy overnight; build anyway.
If you find serenity and happiness, others may be jealous; be happy anyway. The good you do today, people will often forget tomorrow; do good anyway. Give the world the best you have, and it may never be enough; give the world your best anyway. In the final analysis, it is between you and God. It was never between you and them anyway.

Christians, by their choices, their stewardship, and God's will, can find their lives stripped of every material blessing to the point where they can't help but feel at least some self-pity. They may find themselves at the bottom of a hollow pit with nothing and no one, and can be overwhelmed with feelings of hopelessness, of homelessness, of being utterly forsaken all the way down at the bottom. In this state, they can feel like they have been removed from the world, and the world from them.

"Continue in the faith, and saying, 'We must through many tribulations enter the kingdom of God'" (Acts 14:22).

"You endured a great struggle with sufferings ... while you were made a spectacle both by reproaches and tribulations ... you had compassion on me in my chains, and joyfully accepted the plundering of your goods, knowing that you have a better and an enduring possession for yourselves in heaven" (Heb. 10:32–34).

These verses speak of a saint's heart at the highest point of life. The deathly, low-down end is the narrow gate leading to what your spirit has truly desired, to all that the Holy Spirit has been trying to give you: complete joy in Jesus, full and uncrowded, seen through His eyes. In the final analysis, life is between you and God. It is never between you and the world anyway.

This does not mean that physical desolation is the only way to experience clean, free union with God, but it shows the insidious connection we can unfortunately make with the things that keep us from Christ. We may not mean to do that, but it does happen, even when the thing or person we put before the Lord may be good, even a gift that we know He has given us (especially in those cases, it could be argued).

I have experienced an extreme loss and have thought, *At least I still have Jesus.* This has not helped me at all. Immediately I have realized that I am thinking of Christ as virtually the booby prize for the poor loser. I felt like tearing my clothes! The reverse is the only real truth worth hanging on to: Jesus is everything, the One I can't lose, and what I can't keep is nothing compared with Him. Be gone from the heart's desire all but Jesus!

> *But in all things we commend ourselves as ministers*
> *of God: in much patience, in tribulations, in needs,*
> *in distresses, in stripes, in imprisonments, in tumults,*
> *in labors, in sleeplessness, in fastings; by purity, by*
> *knowledge, by longsuffering, by kindness, by the Holy*
> *Spirit, by sincere love, by the word of truth, by the power*
> *of God, by the armor of righteousness on the right hand*
> *and on the left, by honor and dishonor, by evil report*
> *and good report; as deceivers, and yet true; as unknown,*
> *and yet well known; as dying, and behold we live; as*
> *chastened, and yet not killed; as sorrowful, yet always*

rejoicing; as poor, yet making many rich; as having nothing, and yet possessing all things.

—*2 Cor. 6:4–10*

This report is from the apostle Paul, but could be from anyone who will fully do our Father's will. It is natural to work toward a high goal in life and for that goal to involve more money, more ease, and less work. It is natural for us to believe we can somehow keep worldly things as "ours" while maintaining our faith and our relationship to Christ. Our supernatural God calls the supernatural followers of His Son higher—to the lowest place, to be humble recipients "having nothing, and yet possessing all things," content in Him whether with much or with the bare necessities.

Without the Lord's help we will be unable to count our history, our "possessions," and our very life as loss compared with the kind of riches toward which Jesus leads us. We will be unable to change the direction in which we look and travel and the way we see life.

When my family and I were in Egypt for a three-week tour, we were transported all over the countryside by local drivers. *Terrifying* is not too strong of a word for the sensation we felt when we saw what the driving was like there. "Just don't look" became our catchphrase, and a very good one, while sightseeing from the car. This was a warning not to look out the front window at what was looming ahead. We were able to relax and have a good traveling experience seeing Egypt from the side windows of the car.

"Let your eyes look straight ahead, and your eyelids look right before you. Ponder the path of your feet, and let all your ways be established. Do not turn to the right or the left; remove your foot from evil" (Prov. 4:24–27). Through which eyes do we see?

The theory of black holes in space describes the idea of being "drawn in" and virtually consumed by a force so powerful that it's not possible to comprehend, but just mentally attainable enough to cause real amazement and fear. Black holes are supposed to be the darkest of darkness, sucking in even light and not allowing it to escape from their immense gravity. They are an unspeakable freak vacuum from beyond; only God knows where.

The Lord God Almighty has set in motion a continuing transformation of all existence that we call His plan of redemption. This wondrous, unstoppable movement toward a virtually brand-new universe, an existence that can be accomplished only by God, can be viewed as one immense vortex moving all of time, black holes, space, matter, spirit, life, everything of everything, through one place—the cross of Calvary.

Beyond is a holy separation, a recreating of everything and everyone. We know enough about this separation through the Bible to choose which path we will take through this vortex—to what the world's wisdom calls the bottom, then up where we will be exalted to heaven, or down to the top of our man-made way; to eternal life with God or eternal separation from God. Which way are we willing ourselves to go?

In "It's a Long Way Down to the Top," Paul Kossoff wrote:

"I've been playin' rock and roll now about half a million years, and the road to success might be called the trail of tears.

I don't mean to sound bitter; I've surely had my fun. But if I could have looked ahead, I might never have begun.

It's a long way down, so turn your head around. It's a long way down to the top."

It's not necessary to play rock and roll to follow the masses in finding this trail of tears. Any unrestrained seeker who chooses the path of ego by way of the senses in any degree, sooner or later will find that the heart of Christ is the better choice. *Can't I have both? You know, can what I want be allowed by the Lord?* Well, He's the master. Ask Him! When you clean out your heart as the love of Jesus constrains you to make a holy place for Him, do you divide your heart into separate quarters? What do you really want? Can't I have both? He is magnificent; this shouldn't even be a question.

Since the entrance of the Creator God of the universe into time and space, it cannot be denied that Jesus has continually expanded. This growth will continue until He takes over His rightful place, "the fullness of Him who fills all in all" (Eph. 1:23).

In an amazing development, the Spirit of God, who is so incomprehensibly immense that He holds the universe in His hand, assumed flesh and blood to cause conception with one microscopic cell in the womb of a teenage Jewish girl and expanded to be born of water and of blood. We are taught this about Jesus: "Let this mind be in you which was also in Christ Jesus, who, being in the form of God, did not consider it robbery to be equal with God, but made Himself of no reputation, taking the form of a bondservant, and coming in the likeness of men. And being found in appearance as a man, He humbled Himself" (Phil. 2:5–8).

Not only did the omniscient God of all creation expand physically as a human male from birth to death, but he grew mentally, socially, and spiritually as He was raised by His parents, family, friends, and Father in heaven. His role as the Messiah saw Him expand exponentially in the nation of Israel, and after His death, resurrection, and ascension to heaven, He has expanded to the rest of the whole world, day after day, year after year, century after century, until the present. In our time, in the long life of Jesus, He is growing to His ultimate fulfilling of all in all. Make no mistake, He will expand to take His kingship, and the whole universe will have no room left after His filling, and must kneel before Him.

Living in a tempting world that has found a place in our minds and bodies, we must make a significant effort to walk by faith. But we are not saved by effort; we are saved by faith. "This is the work of God, that you believe in Him whom He sent" (John 6:29).

Faith is spiritual, and temptation confronts that faith. In that confrontation, we have a choice to view life like humans or like redeemed divine beings. "Take firm hold of instruction, do not let go; keep her, for she is your life. For they are life to those who find them, and health to all their flesh" (Prov. 4:13, 22). "The words that I speak to you are spirit, and they are life" (John 6:63). "Keep your heart with all diligence, for out of it spring the issues of life" (Prov. 4:23).

Living in this tempting, self-ruled world may look daunting; we may feel the world caressing us like forbidden fruit or scratching at us like determined thorn bushes or worse. But walk we must, and the Holy One walks with us and in us; He alone knows the way and has the eyes for us to see. "The way of the wicked is like darkness; they do not know what makes them stumble. But the path of the just is like the shining sun, that shines ever brighter unto the perfect day" (Prov. 4:18–19)

Charles H. Spurgeon points out our need to "become one with our Foundation."

We are God's permanent, chosen, and grateful possession, specially set aside in this world to remain set aside in this world for His glorification;

'Children of God without fault in the midst of a crooked and perverse generation, among whom you shine as lights in the world' (Phil. 2:15).

The visible practical effect of having undeniably received into our hearts God's immense grace is that we are clearly made into servants of the Lord. To be sure, we are unprofitable and unfaithful servants, but by His blessing grace we are servants. We wear his righteousness to glorify Him only, we are kept alive at his feast of provision for everything He wills, and we show Him we love Him through obeying His commands. He has bought us and freed us from the slave market of sin, adopted us into his family and taught us obedience to His perfect will for our profit. We would serve our Master perfectly if we could, but we don't. We can say like King David, "I am your servant; You have loosed my bonds." Much more, the Lord calls us not just His servants, but His chosen ones—"I have chosen you"; "I have loved you with an everlasting love." Long before existence came into being by the Word of the Lord the names of all His beloved elected ones were written on His heart with the purpose that they would be conformed to the image of Jesus. He foreknew the degree of our stiff-necked will and the evil in our hearts we would succumb to, and yet He made that choice. That eternal choice is a tie that binds our gratitude and His faithfulness which neither party can disown.

If by counting loss for the sake of knowing Jesus we become blind to the tempting desires common to the heaping hordes, then take our eyes of our heart, Lord.

> *Therefore we also, since we are surrounded by so great a cloud of witnesses, let us lay aside every weight, and the sin which so easily ensnares us, and let us run with endurance the race that is set before us, looking unto Jesus, the author and finisher of our faith, who for the joy that was set before Him endured the cross, despising the shame, and has sat down at the right hand of the throne of God. For consider Him who endured such hostility from sinners against Himself, lest you become weary and discouraged in your souls. You have not yet resisted to bloodshed, striving against sin.*

—*Heb. 12:1–4*

The top of the world is a long way down. Self-exaltation almost invariably leads to pride and a long fall. We can't build a platform reliable enough to continuously hold up every aspect of our existence. Worldly riches, fame, social acceptance, and power count for nothing in our exaltation before God. But these things are not the real problem; pride and self-exaltation are. We may amass the world's treasures, dress as pride dictates, and climb atop the heap (ignoring the people we affect in doing so), but Jesus says, "Yet it shall not be so among you; but whoever desires to become great among you, let him be your servant. And whoever desires to be first among you, let him be your slave—just as the Son of Man did not come to be served, but to serve" (Matt. 20:26–28).

"Assuredly, I say to you, unless you are converted and become as little children, you will by no means enter the kingdom of heaven. Therefore whoever humbles himself as this little child is the greatest in the kingdom of heaven" (Matt. 18:3–4). Incredibly, even when we think we have arrived at ground zero and are at last humble, we find that it is still a long way down to divine orientation in God's estimate.

"And indeed there are last who will be first, and there are first who will be last," the Lord says in Luke 13:30. He appears to be referring to the assumption by the Jews that they would receive God's preference as the "first" people of God. In fact, their spiritual pride, their unbelief and poor treatment of their Messiah meant that they would, at least, be moved to the back of the line going into heaven.

In Matthew 20:16, Jesus expands this truth to all believers concerning all things, especially the rewards we sinners may feel we are due. "So the last will be first, and the first last," He says. "For many are called, but few chosen." The Lord is sovereign, not answerable to anyone, and will do as He alone determines.

The system of law (of the world) is easy to figure out: you get what you deserve. The system of grace is foreign to us: God deals with us according to who He is, not according to who we are. With understanding and love, the God of the universe instructs us to stop feeling we deserve anything. "Everyone who exalts himself will be humbled, and he who humbles himself will be exalted" (Luke 18:14).

Some of us may look at life, particularly life without God, and think, *Birth, school, and work are not so bad, but having to make a place and a name for myself in this mess is the worst.* But we are to leave the vision of men by the wayside, seek the Lord in every moment, and leave justice and fairness totally in the purview of God Almighty. Remember, our Lord *is* generosity and infinitely capable of showing it.

▽▲

Imagine making a trip from one destination to another in the kingdom of heaven, on a route that takes more than two days (in our time) to walk. You are not deterred by the length of the trip. You have all of time and then some. Nor do you have to plan your route and keep to it. Whichever way you go, there is no danger or possibility of loss in any form, and no notion that a "correction" will be necessary.

When you decide to stop for however long to do whatever presents itself, if you meet other people, they will be happy to see you and will open their hearts and share whatever they have with you, welcoming you for however long you stay. Everyone is used to this experience; people in heaven know nothing else. They receive and give without even realizing it because nothing is "yours" or "theirs." Everything is the Lord's. Anything and everything are for anyone and everyone all the time. Fatigue will never occur to you, much less affect you, and it is clear that walking is the best possible way to enjoy the Lord, the maximum number of saints along the way, and the perfect, curse-free creation.

Now imagine a conversation about our highway system with a person who has just arrived on earth, maybe even from heaven. This individual is not familiar with earthly life at all and has many questions.

What's the reason for these huge, flat places everywhere and those rolling metal things with people in them? They are a way for people to get from one place to another without going through those areas with barriers around them. *Can they also walk from place to place?* Yes, but over time we have found a way to get from place to place faster and are able to bring other people and things with us. *They go so fast. It looks dangerous and scary. Is there a reason for going so fast?* Most everyone has to get to another place by a certain time, and our time is all filled up, so efficient travel is the way we do it.

What fills up everyone's time, causing all this speed? Our time is mostly filled with working and other activities necessary for life. *So the necessities of life cause this busy-ness.* Here and now they do. *No offense, but a few other parts of your world have very little of this fast pace.* Then perhaps they have a simpler lifestyle. *But here the style is full and fast. Were the other parts of the world like this, changing to a slower life, or has it been the other way around?* In general, life has gotten faster and more filled up everywhere as time passes. *So what are your life and time so filled up with?* Beyond staying alive, we must get clothing for ourselves, find shelter in a living space, fill up the shelter with things to help keep us alive, work to pay for that shelter and buy food and one of those rolling things and other things to entertain us. Then we must buy more clothes and find ways to make more money so we can have more of it all.

Is this what you all do? Most of us. *You don't sound too sure. Don't you speak to each other?* Sometimes, but not all the time, probably because we are so busy. *Did you all agree that this is the preferred way to live?* Not really, but we can see what is happening with each other, and television shows us, too. We do what is common to us. *Someone must have thought of this whole system or figured out how to get to this point.* Maybe, and it's taken a long time to get here. Many people have done very well for themselves by making things and ways to get here. *Really. You are not all the same in the way you live?* No. Some of us have more than others, and that is the main difference to most of us. *So you are all different from each other in the number of things you have.* Yes.

Do you all live together well like this? Well, not as well as could be. Many of the people who have more live differently and in a different place. The same is true for those who have a little, and the same is true for the ones in the middle. *So you are separated by this part of life, and it is all growing faster and fuller and more separate.* So it would seem. *Do you think about life being different, maybe not like it is?* Sometimes, but it is all so big and crazy that it's all most of us can do to try to keep up, or even maintain the necessities.

What are the necessities? They seem to be different for different people. *These rolling things and these highways seem to be necessary because there are so many of them, but not everyone is in one of these machines. Are these people in danger of not surviving?* I don't really know. *But if the highways and rolling things weren't here would anyone survive?* I had not really thought about it, but it seems that in a case like that everything would stop and there would be big trouble. Come to think of it, a lot of our life is relying on things like these.

A comparison of these two scenarios offers a dramatic contrast in mind and heart.

The prophet Isaiah and the apostle Paul had experiences that felt like blast waves from heaven. The result in both cases was that these sinners were immediately cured of their tendency to alter righteous guidelines, even biblical doctrine, to fit a selfish, less-than-pure compromise. Their vision was permanently altered, even if their actions were still subject to the influence of their sinful natures. Must we all go through such a killer shock to enable us to maintain a divine perspective? Let's pray not. Let's put our faith in God and keep our vision latched upon Him with whom all things are possible.

UNTIL THEN

---

*T*O WHAT END IS THE WORLD progressing? Can the eternal be seen amid the temporary, the creation of God amid the work of man? After all the rapid changes of the last fifty years, there still remains in the hearts of most people the yearning for fulfilling activity, rest, peace, and love among men. The drive to achieve a lifetime of fruitful living and to harvest their reward in a time and a manner that offer the intended maximum benefit and enjoyment is a shared motivation in most humans.

Each individual is called to live a life among other individuals. The challenge for each of us is living together, individually. The two notions have attracted and repulsed each other, sometimes simultaneously, for as long as we have been sinners and even for as long as we have been saved sinners.

We don't have to be Gnostic, believing all that is physical and material is a snare to us. It's possible to discern the spiritual in the physical and the eternal beyond the temporary. The gifts of our senses, intellect, and emotions can be recognized as the means of enjoying Jesus in everything and enjoying Him as He is formed inside of us. Conversely, these gifts can separate us from Him, ourselves, and each other.

Because we are called to be holy, it could appear we've been sentenced to life without parole away from our heavenly home in a spiritual land of "Do not touch, do not taste, do not handle" (Col. 2:21). Most certainly this does not have to be so. What is in a man's heart can defile him and bind him alone, but it also can bring cleansing and enormous freedom in a broad place with Christ in him and in those around him.

Another paraphrase of Oswald Chambers:

> As a living witness of God as His child in this world, when sorrow and difficulty come my way, my presenting attitude toward it should not be to ask Him why He did not prevent it, but to pray for His protection so that what He created me to be may remain, and even grow stronger, in spite of the consuming fire of sorrow. Jesus received Himself, knowing His purpose in life and accepting His lot from His Father, inside the fire of sorrow. He wasn't saved from the hour, but in and then out of the hour.

Realizing the love and beauty of our Lord, we move to the thought, "There should be no sorrow!," but there is, and we have to accept that we will be in burning sorrow and receive ourselves from the Lord's hand when He is with us in that sorrow. It is foolish to try to avoid sorrow or to refuse to deal with it. Unfortunately sorrow is one of the most dominant parts of life, and it is no use saying it should not be. Sin, suffering and sorrow are and will be in our lives, and it's not our position or part to say that it's the Lord's mistake in allowing them.

Sorrow produces more depth in a person, but what that depth is then filled with makes a person better or worse. Suffering either gives me to myself or it destroys me. You cannot find or receive yourself through success, because you lose your head over pride. In the daily monotonous routine of life you can't receive yourself because it is blocked as you give in to complaining. The only discovery of our real self is in the fires of sorrow. Why so? Why it is this way is of no substantial importance; it is true in Scripture and in human experience. When someone has been through this fire and come out with his real self, you can always recognize it and come to him with your need, being confident in him to have time for you. But if not, the person who lacks this experience will not have time for you and turn you away, probably in contempt. If you will receive yourself in the fires of sorrow, God will make you nourishment for other people.

"What shall I say? 'Father, save Me from this hour'? But for this purpose I came to this hour. 'Father, glorify Your name'" (John 12:27–28).

We do and experience many things, but must this happen by ourselves? Were we not intended to be with another One in these experiences? Is not all experience from the hand of our intimately constant, perfect companion?

The invisibility of this beloved One is irrelevant. In our memories, don't we feel the embrace of our beloved flesh-and-blood human treasures and clearly see their faces? I do. That feeling by way of memory is infinitely more available than actually seeing their faces and embracing them; it's available at will. God's presence is more real and available than the physical and far more tangible than memory. We perceive this world and live in it by ourselves only because we choose to neglect the spiritual in the physical and the eternal beyond the temporary. There is immense joy to be found and wise warning to be heeded.

For all the time on earth man has had and all he has done to make life "good, better, best," God has always been the very best, the creator and giver of life.

In "It's Alright, Ma (I'm Only Bleeding)," Bob Dylan sings, "Disillusioned words like bullets bark / as human gods aim for their mark / make everything from toy guns that spark / to flesh-colored Christs that glow in the dark / It's easy to see without looking too far that not much is really sacred."

Is this just all one man's idea? To relate wisdom from the Lord through Oswald Chambers again;

"Read John 17. Jesus has prayed that you 'may be one' with the Father as He is. Are you helping God to answer that prayer, or do you have some other goal for your life? Since you became a disciple, you cannot be as independent as you used to be."

During all the time we have pursued distracting shiny objects for our "self" and warred against each other to acquire and keep these idols as our miserable replacements for the Lord in His rightful place of preeminence within us and around us, God has graciously used our things, systems, and "achievements" as tools to work out our redemption. We certainly cannot fathom the perfection of His work and the complex, amazing control the Lord exercises as He brings all creation to the time of His heavenly kingdom. Our neediness will become still, and we will gain perfect satisfaction and peace of mind in Christ when we let go of worldly questions, doubts, and desires, persevering until "in that day you will ask Me nothing" (John 16:23).

By God's grace and an abiding heart, we can look at the enemy and see that our King has won, that the world will be made new, and that we are to be sanctified instruments of His glorious plan in what looks like a hopeless mess to so many.

"Arise, and do not be afraid" (Matt. 17:7). "Arise, go your way. Your faith has made you well" (Luke 17:19). "But that the world may know that I love the Father, and as the Father gave Me commandment, so I do. Arise, let us go from here" (John 14:31).

Do you have a yearning for Jesus and such an overwhelming hope in His promise of heaven that you see by faith His glorious kingdom breaking through the enemy's wall of lies (the world system)? Do you see the light of the world that is coming soon, breaking through the cracks—the cracks in the sidewalk, the cracks at the edges of people's smiles, the cracks in your Bible, the cracks left by the enemies' darts, the cracks in your resolve, the cracks in pride everywhere? Do you see Jesus' light through holes that almost everyone else does not see for the gloss of today's media, narcissism, and "We can do it!" self-sufficiency?

Finally, if this book has recalled whatever things are true, noble, just, pure, lovely, of good report, of any virtue, of anything praiseworthy (Phil. 4:8), if it brings to remembrance that our real treasure is in heaven and that we are to "seek first the kingdom of God and His righteousness, and all these things shall be added to you," then although the way is narrow, it won't be long now to the everlasting top. That is indeed a good report.

Even my heart wants to hear just the good news that Jesus has saved me to be with Him in heaven, but even the goods news in my heart can be so only if there is corresponding bad news to be overcome. Otherwise, as the popular culture says, "It's all good!"

The reader can contemplate all this and come to a personal decision or just forget about it, which is also a decision. I have attempted to open the eyes of our hearts to serious observation and to ask whether the ways of this world are normal or not. Before the fall, I believe most ways of our present world would not have been perceived as normal but as abominable. These ways will cease to exist in heaven. Does this matter, presently, in discerning what we are willing to mix with the commandment "to be holy as I am holy"? Walk in the light of His Word by prayer and with a singularity of will to be like Jesus and to see Him in paradise.

We sojourn individually together through this life of choice.

"Repent, for the kingdom of heaven is at hand" (Matt 4:17).

BIBLIOGRAPHY

Oswald Chambers, *The Complete Works of Oswald Chambers* (Grand Rapids: Oswald Chambers Publications Associations, Ltd., 2000).

A. W. Tozer, *The Best of A. W. Tozer, Book Two* (Camp Hill: Wing Spread Publishers, 2007).

Charles H. Spurgeon, *Morning and Evening* (Wheaton: Crossways Books, 2003).